HOW TO ANSWER
INTERVIEW QUESTIONS
EASY AND COMPREHENSIVE STEP BY STEP GUIDE TO
LANDING A JOB

ROBERT L. WHITE Ph.D

Book design by (The casmirs)

Cover design by (The casmirs)

thecasmirs@gmail.com

First Edition: January, 2024

ABOUT THE AUTHOR

Dr. Robert L. White is a distinguished author, entrepreneur, and expert in Business and Human Resources management. With a wealth of experience and academic prowess, Dr. White has positioned himself as a thought leader in the field, offering valuable insights to individuals seeking success in their professional journeys.

Dr. Robert L. White has earned a Ph.D. in Business and Human Resources management, showcasing a commitment to academic excellence and a deep understanding of the intricate dynamics of business operations and human capital management.

At the helm of a successful business, Dr. White has demonstrated an exemplary ability to navigate the complexities of the business world. His leadership has undoubtedly played a pivotal role in the growth and prosperity of the enterprise.

In addition to his role in the business sector, Dr. White holds significant positions as both the Board Chairman and a distinguished member of multinational recruiting firms. This dual role affords him a unique perspective, combining leadership at the strategic level with hands-on involvement in the recruitment industry.

Dr. White's expertise lies at the intersection of business strategy and human resources management. His profound knowledge in these areas is not only reflected in his academic achievements but is also evident in the success of the business he leads and his contributions to multinational recruiting firms.

As the author of the book "How to Answer Job Interview Questions: Easy and Comprehensive Step-by-Step Guide to Landing a Job," Dr. White extends his expertise to a broader audience. The book is a testament to his commitment to empowering individuals with the knowledge and skills needed to navigate the competitive landscape of job interviews successfully.

Beyond his entrepreneurial endeavors, Dr. White's roles as the Board Chairman and a member of multinational recruiting firms underscore his commitment to shaping the future of the business landscape. These leadership positions position him as a key influencer in decision-making processes at both organizational and industry levels.

In his multifaceted career, Dr. Robert L. White has not only demonstrated a keen understanding of the intricacies of business and human resources but has actively contributed to the growth and development of individuals and organizations alike. His leadership, academic achievements, and authorship collectively paint a portrait of an individual dedicated to fostering success and excellence in the professional realm.

Table of Contents

INTRODUCTION

Embarking on a career-defining journey, the ability to navigate and conquer job interviews is a skill that can elevate your professional trajectory. In today's competitive job market, where opportunities abound but so do qualified candidates, the mastery of answering interview questions is akin to wielding a powerful tool that sets you apart. This comprehensive guide is your compass in this uncharted territory, promising to unravel the intricacies of responding to interview queries with precision, eloquence, and confidence.

Why Mastering Interview Questions is Crucial
The interview process is the crucible where your qualifications, experiences, and aspirations are put to the test. It is not just a perfunctory step in the hiring process; it is a pivotal moment that can determine the trajectory of your career. At its core, the importance of mastering interview questions lies in the profound impact it has on your ability to communicate effectively, showcase your suitability for the role, and stand out amidst a sea of talented candidates.

A well-crafted response is not merely a regurgitation of facts from your resume but a strategic presentation of your professional narrative. It is an opportunity to articulate your unique value proposition, demonstrate your problem-solving abilities, and showcase the soft skills that make you an ideal fit for the organization. Mastering interview questions is about transforming what could be perceived as a grueling interrogation into a compelling conversation where you, as the interviewee, take center stage.

This book explores the psychological and practical aspects of interviews, shedding light on how your responses shape the interviewer's perception of you. From the strategic selection of examples to the art of storytelling, this book provides insights into the nuances that can turn an ordinary interview into an extraordinary opportunity.

Understanding the importance of mastering interview questions empowers you to approach each interaction with intentionality. It's not merely about answering questions; it's about crafting a narrative that resonates, engages, and leaves a lasting impression. As we navigate through the intricacies of effective communication, you'll gain the tools to transform the interview from a challenge into a platform to showcase your professional prowess.

Overview of the Interview Process
Beyond the significance of individual questions lies the broader landscape of the interview process. Navigating this process requires a strategic understanding of its stages, expectations, and potential pitfalls. Imagine the interview as a theatrical production, with each stage

contributing to the unfolding narrative of your professional story.

This section serves as your script, your backstage pass to the production that is your job interview journey. It begins with the initial application, where your resume and cover letter take center stage. The script then transitions to the screening stage, involving phone interviews and potentially video assessments. The plot thickens with in-person interviews, potentially extending to second or third-round evaluations, and culminates in the dramatic finale—the offer or the regretful rejection.

Understanding the dynamics of the interview process equips you with the knowledge to prepare effectively at each stage. It's about anticipating the director's cues, knowing when to deliver a powerful monologue and when to engage in a dynamic dialogue. Different companies adopt varied interview formats—traditional one-on-one sessions, behavioral assessments, technical evaluations, case studies—and this chapter acts as your guide, demystifying each format and providing insights into what to expect.

As we journey through the stages of the interview process, you'll gain a holistic understanding of the challenges and opportunities each phase presents. Armed with this knowledge, you'll be better prepared to navigate the twists and turns, ensuring that you not only survive the production but emerge as the star performer.

Setting the Stage for Success

Success in job interviews is not a stroke of luck but a result of meticulous preparation and a strategic mindset. Setting the stage for success involves a holistic approach that goes beyond answering questions. It encompasses everything from researching the company and the role to crafting a compelling resume and portfolio.

This chapter is your backstage guide to the prelude of the interview—the preparation phase. It begins with the foundation: researching the company and the role you're applying for. Knowing the ins and outs of the organization, its culture, and the specific requirements of the role is not just a formality; it's a strategic advantage.

Crafting a compelling resume and portfolio is the next act in this preparation phase. Your resume is not merely a list of qualifications; it's a marketing document that sells your skills and experiences. Similarly, your portfolio is a visual representation of your capabilities, a tangible showcase of what you bring to the table.

Anticipating and addressing potential red flags is the final touch in setting the stage for success. It's about proactively addressing gaps in employment, career transitions, or any other aspect of your professional history that might raise eyebrows. This chapter provides you with the tools to turn potential weaknesses into strengths, ensuring that you present a cohesive and compelling narrative.

The journey to mastering interview questions begins with an understanding of why it is crucial, navigates through the intricacies of the interview process, and culminates in setting the stage for success. Each element is a crucial piece of the puzzle, contributing to your overall readiness to face the challenges and opportunities that job interviews present. As we embark on this exploration, remember that mastery is not just about skill; it's about mindset, preparation, and the ability to seize the spotlight when it matters most.

CHAPTER 2

UNDERSTANDING THE INTERVIEW LANDSCAPE

An interview can be intimidating, regardless of whether this is your first time applying for a job or you're trying to move companies.

It's crucial to keep in mind that the job interview process is an excellent chance to hone and showcase your marketing and critical thinking abilities to promote yourself and your work in the best possible light. Similar to any other pitch, you must be aware of your target, be succinct, and make it obvious what you have to offer.

This chapter acts as your compass, offering a thorough overview of the many aspects of job interviews, including the varied forms interviews might take, the kinds of interviews you may encounter, and the responsibilities that different interviewers play.

The Role of Different Interviewers: HR, Hiring Managers, Technical Experts
A varied group of interviewers choreographs complex acts

during job interviews. Every member of this ensemble is essential to assessing your candidacy from a distinct angle. Comprehending the distinct functions of several interviewers—HR specialists, Hiring Managers, and Technical Experts—is crucial for customizing your answers to align with their particular anticipations.

The HR Professional: Gatekeeper of Company Culture
In the employment process, human resources specialists act as the first gatekeepers. They do more than just review applications; they are defenders of the corporate culture, making sure that applicants share the organization's values and ethos in addition to having the necessary abilities.

Key Respondsibilities
Cultural Fitness: HR specialists conduct a cultural fit assessment to see if your values, mission, and work culture match those of the organization. Your preferred method of collaboration, work style, and adaptability may be the subjects of questions.

Checking for Fundamental Requirements: They check that your credentials meet the job specifications and could also ask you questions about your background in the workforce, your degree, and your general suitability for the role.

Communication Skills Evaluation: Your ability to express yourself effectively and professionally is evaluated, as HR is frequently the first point of contact.

Success Strategies:
Research the Company's Culture: In your answers, show that you are aware of the company's beliefs and culture.

Emphasize Soft Skills: Emphasize your teamwork, communication, and flexibility abilities to demonstrate how well you fit into the company's culture.
Professionalism is Essential: Upholding a professional manner is essential for HR professionals, as they frequently serve as the company's face.

The Hiring Manager: Architect of Team Dynamics
During the interview process, hiring managers play a pivotal role and have significant control over the outcome. They are essential in forming the dynamics of the team because they make sure the chosen applicant fits the current structure of the team while also fulfilling the technical requirements.

Key Respondsibilities
Technical and Managerial Competency Evaluation: Hiring managers concentrate on your managerial, if appropriate, and technical skills. Your experience, problem-solving skills, and leadership style may be the topics of inquiry.

Team Fit Evaluation: They determine how well you would fit in with the current group. Your capacity to resolve conflicts, work well with others, and foster a pleasant team environment may all be explored in the questions that follow.

Alignment with Departmental Objectives: Hiring managers assess your knowledge of the department's objectives and the ways in which your work helps to achieve them.

Success Strategies:
Dynamics of Research Teams: To ensure that your comments are appropriate, be aware with the department's objectives, the team structure, and ongoing projects.

Emphasize Experience That Is Relevant: Highlight prior experiences that demonstrate your capacity to effectively interact and contribute to team objectives.

Showcase Your Leadership Skills: If appropriate for the role, provide examples of your leadership responsibilities or successful team outcomes.

Technical Experts: Evaluators of Proficiency and Problem-Solving
Technical experts evaluate your competence in the particular abilities needed for the job. These experts are frequently specialists in a given sector. In fields like information technology, engineering, or science where specific knowledge is required, their function is vital.

Primary Responsibility:

Technical experts analyze your technical proficiency by asking you specific questions and perhaps using practical tests.

Evaluation of Problem-Solving and Analytical Skills: To gauge your analytical thinking and problem-solving prowess, they might show you case studies or scenarios.

Comprehensive Knowledge Exploration: Technical Experts probe your comprehension of ideas, practices, and new trends that are unique to your sector.

Success Strategy:

Examine the technical concepts: Review terms, ideas, and current advancements unique to the business to show that you are knowledgeable.

Display Real-World Use: Give instances from your professional experience when you have used technical expertise to solve issues or advance initiatives.

Stress the need for ongoing learning: Emphasize the times you've attended pertinent workshops, sought out further qualifications, or kept up with changes in the field.

It is possible to customize your comments by being aware of the differences between the jobs of Technical Experts, Hiring Managers, and HR experts. Remember that every interviewer brings a different viewpoint to the table and that addressing their specific concerns helps strengthen your application as a whole. A comprehensive plan for interview success is created when you wow HR with culture alignment, resonate with the hiring manager's vision and demonstrate your technical acumen to experts.

Common Interview Formats and Structures

Going into a job interview is like walking onto a dynamic stage, where the scenes might change significantly from one to the next. The interview process incorporates a range of styles and procedures rather than being a one-size-fits-all situation. This chapter provides you with a thorough overview of the typical interview structures and formats that you may come across in the course of your career.

Traditional One-on-One Interviews: The Classic Dialogue

Conventional one-on-one interviews, which reflect the traditional conversation between an interviewer and a candidate, are the cornerstone of the hiring process. This approach makes it possible to have a more personal discussion and get a better sense of the candidate's background, character, and experiences.

In a standard interview, you and one other person meet to go over your qualifications and experience for the position for which you are applying. This person is usually a manager, recruiter, or human resources (HR) representative. In a conventional interview, you meet the interviewer at the company, and the interview takes place in a conference room or an office. They might question you about your training, professional background, and suitability for the position.

Important attributes:
Individual Focus: To enable tailored communication, each candidate has an individual interview session with the interviewer.

Diverse Questions: The questions offer a comprehensive picture of the individual, ranging from behavioral questions to technical evaluations.

Adaptability: The format is a mainstay of the interview process since it can be readily tailored to a variety of professions and sectors.

Tips for Success.
Create a rapport with the interviewer by demonstrating your amiability and excitement for the position.

Storytelling: Create gripping tales that highlight your accomplishments, experiences, and capacity for problem-solving.

Active Listening: To show off your ability to communicate effectively, pay close attention and respond to questions during the interview.

Panel Interviews: Navigating the Group Dynamics
Panel interviews require candidates to confront several interviewers at once, each of whom represents a distinct aspect of the hiring process. In businesses where a variety of viewpoints are essential to the decision-making process, this approach is typical.

A group of people from the firm or organization interview you in a panel (or committee) interview. The interview is set up so that the same people ask the same questions of every candidate to maintain impartiality. Interviewers may include HR officials, colleagues, and/or your prospective supervisor(s). Large businesses or organizations are most likely to use panel interviews.

Note down the names and work titles of the interviewers as they introduce themselves at the start of the interview. Try to maintain eye contact with each panelist as you respond to their questions during the interview. Whether the interviewer is a manager or a staff assistant, you should always regard their inquiries with the same importance.

Being the interviewer for a panel can be demanding because there are a lot of questions to answer. But, from the standpoint of the employer, this kind of interview is beneficial since it demonstrates your ability to communicate with a range of individuals and gives the interviewers a chance to share their opinions about your performance.

Important attributes:
Diverse Viewpoints: To provide a thorough assessment, panel members frequently include representatives from HR, management, and particular departments.

Time Management: It can be more efficient for interviewers and candidates to do a single panel interview as opposed to several one-on-one meetings.

Stress Test: To gauge a candidate's flexibility and poise, they must manage interactions with several interviewers.

Tips for Success
Talk to Each Panelist: Make sure you speak with each panelist separately and acknowledge their contribution to the hiring process.

Keep Eye Contact: Make sure you keep eye contact with each member of the panel to project professionalism and confidence.

Structure Your Comments: Make sure that each panelist receives a clear understanding of your qualifications and suitability by clearly organizing your comments.

Sequential (Serial) Interviews: A Gradual Unveiling
Candidates move through a series of one-on-one meetings with various interviewers or interview panels in sequential interviews. Every meeting builds on the one before it, revealing more and more about the candidate's background and suitability for the position.

Important attributes:
Layered Evaluation: Every interviewer concentrates on a different facet of the candidate's profile, adding to a thorough evaluation.

In-Depth Exploration: To provide a nuanced review, candidates may be asked a range of questions, from behavioral queries to technical assessments.

Progressive Insights: With each interview, the sequential format enables interviewers to probe further into the candidate's background and skills.

Tips for Success
Response Consistency: To offer a credible and cohesive story, be sure that your responses are consistent from one session to the next.

Flexibility: Adjust your answers to each interviewer's unique issues and be ready for a variety of interview formats.

Follow-up Questions: Based on your previous responses, you should prepare to answer further questions from other interviewers.

Behavioral Interviews: Probing Past Experiences
The main goal of behavioral interviews is to evaluate a candidate's historical handling of particular circumstances. The foundation of this style is the idea that performance in the future may be reliably predicted from past behavior.

A behavioral interview will be conducted with the great majority of interview candidates. Behavioral inquiries are based on the idea that previous behavior is a reliable predictor of future behavior and therefore concentrate on past performances rather than hypothetical scenarios.

Researching the business and your interviewer will help you get ready for this type of interview. To refresh your memory of the requirements the company has set, it can also be beneficial to go over the job description. As you prepare your answers to frequently asked interview questions, consider the skills and duties the employer might bring up.

The four common questions for behavioral interviews are as follows:

Which of your projects was the hardest to finish? Tell me about it.
Who was the hardest client you have ever assisted? Tell me about the circumstances.

Which class did you find the most difficult? Tell me why you found it difficult.
Have you ever been a part of a group? What was the purpose of the team project, what was your involvement, and did everything go well or was there a problem? What was the project's outcome?
You can successfully respond to behavioral questions by using the following strategies:

Never bring up unfavorable remarks about your previous supervisors, instructors, or clients. Even if a certain person was challenging, talk about the challenge and the affirmation you had once you were able to fulfill it instead.

Make an effort to project an eager and upbeat image of a problem solver. Someone who was mistreated or didn't get along with the team in general won't pique the curiosity of interviewers.

Provide direct answers to questions with a start, middle, and end to your response.

Whenever you can, try to quantify your responses. If you were questioned about your employment managing the school library, for instance, state how many volumes you oversee each day—ten, one hundred, or one thousand, for instance. Estimating is OK.

Make sure your response is related to the final result. Using the library example once more, you may respond by saying that there was a 75% reduction in missing books when the electronic checkout system was used.
To prevent yourself from straying, keep your attention on the subject posed.
If you believe you have strayed from the topic or if you are unsure about the question, ask the interviewer to repeat it.

Important Attributes:
Interviewers use structured questions to elicit instances of past experiences from candidates, highlighting particular actions and results.

Assessment of Competencies: The objective is to assess important competencies like leadership, flexibility, problem-solving, and teamwork.

STAR approach: To organize their answers and give a thorough account of their prior experiences, candidates frequently employ the STAR approach (Situation, Task, Action, Result).

Tips for Success
Prepare Examples: Be ready with examples from your work history that showcase pertinent competencies in response to often-asked behavioral inquiries.

Measure Your Outcomes: To offer hard proof of your contributions, measure your former experiences' accomplishments and results.

Demonstrate Your Growth: If you've encountered difficult circumstances, highlight the lessons you took away and how you've evolved.

Technical Interviews: Assessing Skills and Competencies
In fields like information technology, engineering, or science where specialized skills are needed, technical interviews are a must. During these interviews, a candidate's aptitude for using technical knowledge in practical situations is evaluated.

To some extent, all interviews are technical, especially those for technical employment. However some interview formats prioritize asking precise technical questions above asking broad questions about you, your experience, your objectives, etc. Information technology, computer science, and computer engineering are the fields that most frequently conduct interviews that heavily emphasize technical knowledge.

It will be difficult for you to answer the technical interview questions without drawing on your understanding of particular technological programs, processes, and procedures. These are a few typical questions for technical interviews:

1. Which tools have you used for development?
2. Which languages have you worked with in programming?
3. Which tools have you used for source control?
4. Give an instance of how you have practically used your technical expertise.
5. What components, and why, are essential to a successful team?
6. Which technical qualifications do you hold, and how do you keep them up to date?

Technical interviews may also consist of "brain teaser" questions, which ask you to solve a technical problem using your knowledge and experience; "how-to" questions, which explain how to carry out a technical procedure; or "what-if" questions, which pose hypothetical scenarios and ask you to explain how you would handle them.

You must possess a comprehensive understanding of the company's or organization's operations and technology landscape to speak with assurance about your technical proficiency in those domains. Additionally, it's critical to demonstrate how you can apply your knowledge to address practical issues and to explain your expertise in a way that is understandable to non-technical individuals.

Important Attributes:
Problem-Solving Scenarios: To demonstrate their problem-solving skills, candidates frequently face real-world issues or coding challenges.
Comprehensive Knowledge Evaluation: Interviewers evaluate a candidate's comprehension of technical terms, procedures, and instruments.
Interactive Assessments: In certain technical interviews, candidates are given practical tasks to demonstrate their abilities in real-time.
Success Advice:

Examine Technical Concepts: Give careful consideration to every technical concept, tool, and methodology that pertains to the position.

Practice addressing problems: Take part in coding challenges or fake technical interviews to improve your ability to solve problems under time constraints.

It's All About Communication: Even in the face of difficulties, be sure to express your ideas and methods for overcoming problems clearly and concisely.

Case Interviews: Solving Real-World Challenges

Case interviews, which are common in consulting and business strategy roles, expose candidates to actual company situations. The objective is to evaluate the applicant's capacity for analytical thought, problem-solving abilities, and application of theoretical knowledge to real-world scenarios.

Though they are occasionally utilized in a variety of industries, including financial services, healthcare, consumer products, and education, case interviews are mostly used in management consulting. An interviewee is supposed to provide solutions for a fictitious business challenge, or case, during a case interview. The case evaluates the interviewee's knowledge and abilities in several areas, including analysis, reasoning, problem-solving techniques, math, accounting, and economics, understanding of a particular industry, communication, creativity, and the capacity to perform under pressure.

In case interviews, brief questions to gauge a market's size may be asked:

1. How many adolescent females purchased Gucci bracelets during the summer?
2. In December, how many Christmas trees are sold in New York?

3. In Manchester, how many disposable cameras are bought each month?

The interviewer wants you to estimate a final response based on several pieces of data, not an exact figure (e.g., the population of the United States). In order to assess how you organize a problem, the interviewer wants you to deconstruct this broad request into more manageable steps that can be calculated. Your ability to operate under pressure and your proficiency in basic math are also being tested by the interviewer.

Keep in mind that the interviewer is more interested in seeing the method you use to approximate the answer than in receiving a precise response.

In-depth questioning regarding a specific problem pertaining to operations or strategy may take up to 45 minutes during a case interview. Someone might ask you how to handle a make-believe classroom setting. You can be required to streamline procedures in a medical situation. Data regarding the business or sector of the economy related to the query posed might be provided to you. Charts, accounting statements, or other background information may be requested of you, like in the case of the following questions: 1. An Austin, Texas, neighborhood toy store is being considered for acquisition by the CEO of a well-known national toy manufacturer. 2. How would you suggest the CEO decide whether to buy the store?

After that, you can receive additional details on the national toy firm or be asked to request what you require. The interviewer is assessing you in part because of the questions you ask, which indicate the kinds of information you believe are crucial to consider before making a purchasing choice. You are attempting to determine whether the acquisition and integration of the neighborhood business will be profitable in the long run, and if not, how well the neighborhood shop fits into the overall plan of the national corporation.

Case interview sessions are provided by extracurricular consulting groups or career services at many schools. Except for management consulting positions, case interviews are extremely uncommon and differ greatly from traditional job interviews. Thus, unless you are interested in working as a management consultant, don't waste any time getting ready for case interviews. Practice with case interviews is essential if you wish to work in management consulting. A consulting firm will not hire you if you cannot complete multiple case interviews.

Important Attributes:
Business Scenarios: Applicants are required to analyze, strategize, and provide solutions to a given business challenge or situation.

Interactive Discussion: The candidate and the interviewer frequently engage in a lively exchange of ideas during the interview.

Organized Approach: Applicants should present a methodical and analytical approach to problem-solving by organizing their answers rationally.

Tips for Success
Get Acquainted with Case Structures: To get comfortable with different kinds of business circumstances, practice with different case forms.

Systematic Problem-Solving: Stress a methodical and organized approach to problem-solving, showcasing your capacity to deconstruct intricate problems.

Clarity of Communication: Talk about your ideas clearly and concisely, and participate in a cooperative conversation with the interviewer.

Group Interviews: Collaborative Evaluation
In group interviews, several candidates are evaluated at the same time, with a focus on their capacity for effective teamwork, communication, and contribution. This structure is typical in fields where collaboration is essential.

During a group interview, a company or organization's support staff, HR representatives, and potential supervisors meet with a group of job hopefuls concurrently. Group interviews not only offer an effective way to present material to a large number of candidates at once, but they also allow interviewers to see how candidates behave under pressure and interact with one another. In-person group interviews are more common than those conducted online.

A group interview can be conducted in several ways:
A. Presentation by the employer about the business or organization is followed by a group Q&A session.

B. Problem-solving exercise where candidates collaborate to provide one or more answers to a hypothetical scenario that the employer presents

C. Collaborative work-related exercise that candidates must figure out how to complete in a group

Interviewers keep a close eye on candidates' analytical, interpersonal, leadership (including the capacity to persuade and inspire others), communication, and stress-handling abilities. They also search for nonverbal cues that convey a message, such as smiling, that is favorable or negative, such as rolling their eyes or fiddling with their hair. During a group interview, pay attention to your body language. Anxious people are prone to giving the wrong impression!

Important attributes:
Interactive Dynamics: Applicants take part in cooperative activities, problem-solving sessions, and group discussions.

Observation of Interpersonal Skills: Interviewers evaluate candidates based on how they collaborate, exchange ideas, and support team goals.

Leadership Assessment: Candidates' capacity for teamwork, navigating group dynamics, and leadership may be assessed through observation.

Tips for Success
Harmony, Cooperation and Individual Contribution: Make an effort to strike a balance between participating in group activities and giving others the space to voice their opinions.

Good Communication: Express yourself clearly, pay attention to what other people are saying, and have productive conversations.

Display Leadership Qualities: When the chance arises, show off your leadership abilities by assuming charge of situations or organizing team activities.

Video and Phone Interviews: Overcoming Distant
With the rise of remote work, phone and video interviews are becoming more and more popular. Employers can evaluate applicants using these formats without having to speak with them in person.
Important attributes:
Communication Flexibility: Candidates should emphasize engagement, clarity, and tone while communicating virtually.

Technical Readiness: Make sure you have a reliable internet connection, working audio and visual gear, and know how to use the video conferencing software that you have selected.

Focused Interaction: Since there are fewer nonverbal signs available, verbal communication and expressive language must receive more attention.

Tips for Success
Practice Technical Setup: Make sure your camera, microphone, and internet connection are operating without a hitch by running test runs.

Establish a formal setting: For the interview, pick a place that is calm and well-lit to reduce distractions and provide a polished background.

Keep Eye Contact: Looking straight into the camera during a virtual interview communicates attention to detail and active participation.

Informal Interviews
By definition, informational interviews allow you to learn more about the field you're thinking about pursuing. Your session will go more smoothly if you are well-prepared, because the finest informational interviews are two-way discussions that resemble conversations rather than interrogations. You and your interviewer will gain from

the time spent together, and your research will enable you to communicate important information with them.

Certain questions in an informative interview center on the interviewer:

1. How did you enter this field, company, or sector of the economy?
2. What appeals to you most about it? What has yielded the greatest rewards?
3. What presents the most challenge? Did you find anything surprising?
4. How would a normal day, week, or month go?
5. Which abilities are the most important to possess, cultivate, and keep up to succeed?
6. Which personality types tend to succeed the best?
7. What knowledge do you now possess that you wish you had at the beginning? It's an excellent idea to pose this question because it makes people consider their professional path. (People find this inquiry to be unexpected and appreciate it.)

In addition to helping you delve deeper and discover more about the position, the field, and the career, these kinds of questions build rapport.

A few questions for an informational interview center on work and career:

My study indicates that [name the competition] is the leading rival. Am I overlooking somebody important, in your opinion? Is there a recent player that I should be aware of?

I've read that [insert name of trend, challenge, or innovation] is a significant innovation, trend, or challenge. Does this have an impact on your company or job? Is the media exaggerating this? Are there any other inventions, trends, or issues that I should be aware of?

Although it's not the primary consideration when accepting a job, I'd like to know more about compensation. I've read that [name pay range] and [name lifestyle, travel, and work culture] are typical for people in this position. Is that correct? Existing subtleties to this that the mainstream media hasn't covered?

It is typical for people in this position to have [name experiences and skills], based on my study. Is [summarizing your experience and skills] a competitive background for me? Would you consider me for a vacancy in your group? What actions can I take to increase my chances?

If it isn't made clear in their introduction or on their business card, what department are you in?
Who is in charge of this division?

What role does it play in the organization as a whole?
Is this the standard setup, or are your rivals set up differently?

I'm attempting to find out who manages the [name department you want] while researching [name another organization]. Are you aware of someone I could speak with there?

This is possibly the most crucial question to ask during an informative interview:

I intend to talk to [name the people] right now. Who else ought to be on my list? If I were to contact them, might I use your name?

Typical informational interviews go between thirty and forty-five minutes, and they can be an important component of your research to make sure you are focusing on the correct kinds of positions.

As you maneuver across the varied terrain of typical interview forms and frameworks, keep in mind that readiness, flexibility, and a methodical approach are crucial. Understanding the subtleties of each style will improve your overall performance in the interview by giving you a unique opportunity to highlight your qualifications, abilities, and personality. Make sure your preparation is tailored to the particular requirements of the interview style. You should approach each scenario with passion, confidence, and a readiness to perform well.

CHAPTER 2

PREPARING FOR SUCCESSFUL INTERVIEW

Success in any endeavor, including job interviews, is largely dependent on preparation. A carefully considered and comprehensive preparation plan serves as your compass when you enter the interview room, helping you navigate tricky situations and making sure you give the best possible impression.

Doing your homework about possible employers is essential to a successful job hunt. Three crucial points in a job search are when this study is useful: first, when you are choosing the type of firm you want to work for; second, when you are prepared to apply; and third, during the interview, when your familiarity with the business is tested.

This chapter explores the many facets of getting ready for success, from studying the business and the position to creating an effective portfolio and resume to creating a customized interview plan.

Examining the Organization and the Position

You may greatly enhance your chances of acing the interview by doing some research on the company ahead of time. Interviews can be anxious and stressful, but one of the best ways to feel more prepared and secure in your responses is to do some research on the company before the interview. You will approach your next interviews with the appropriate mindset if you do this.

It will also demonstrate your familiarity with the business and your excitement for the position.

Finding out about the company's goals and culture when conducting research for interviews will also help you determine if this is the perfect fit for you. It's crucial to select interview subjects that fascinate and excite you.

Refuse to take a job from an employer whose principles diverge from your own.

You don't want to work for a firm that doesn't fit you; therefore, doing your homework is essential to avoiding the risk of leaving too soon.

What to Research Before an Interview?

Are you unsure about how to look up firms to interview for a job before applying? Are you aware of the things to look up about a company before an interview?

The following are some important things to learn from your research:

1. What the business does, the sector in which it works, and its location
2. The approximate number of members on the team
3. The company's background, significant accomplishments, and pivotal times
4. Customers, clientele, or target market of the business
5. The sector in which the business works New goods or services that the business has introduced
6. The mission, ambitions, objectives, or goals of the company

Now that you are aware of exactly what to look up before a job interview, let's see how to do some research on the company:

How to Research Companies for Interviews
1. Go to the business's website
Since researching jobs is now easier than ever, your initial step should be to search online.

Check out the employer's website's home page, "About Us," and "Meet The Team" sections to learn more about the company's offerings, history, accomplishments, news, and team details.

Check out the mission statement of the company here as well!

Keep an eye out for any recurring themes, messages, or ideals on the website.

Maybe there's a lot of information about ethical guidelines, or perhaps company culture is well highlighted.

These factors will influence how you see the company and the qualities that they value in a candidate.

Investigate a firm in-depth, taking note of its past business names and the names of its directors and CEO, and use Companies House to perform some research. The next step is to write down the aspects of this company that particularly attract you.

Did they just recently launch? Do they work in an industry about which you have strong feelings? Do you find the business culture appealing? Remember these things so you can bring them up in your graduate job interview.

2. Look up the Company on Social Media
Most businesses have a social media presence.

You may learn a lot about a firm and some of its important players from its feeds on YouTube, Instagram, Facebook, Twitter, and LinkedIn.

Clients of the business may be found on LinkedIn, and their corporate culture can be found on Instagram.

Please click "like" or "follow" the firm to see what they are posting and to be informed of the most recent news.

Mentioning during the interview that you followed them on social media and saw their most recent news demonstrates excellent initiative and can make a big impression on an employer.

If you are familiar with the interviewees, look up their profiles on LinkedIn to learn more about their experience, hobbies, and functions.

With this information, you can strike up a discussion and talk about any shared hobbies to build rapport while being proactive!

3. Check out company review websites
Websites such as Glassdoor, The Job Crowd, and Crunchbase offer essential information about a company, including its workforce size, along with company biographies and reviews from former employees.

You can prepare your replies by reviewing the questions that candidates for similar graduate posts were asked during their interviews.

Reviews can also help you learn more about the culture of the business and what to expect from the leadership.

Look for accomplishments and pivotal occasions (e.g., did the business just obtain a sizable amount of funding?) as these will be very impressive to the employer if you bring them up during the interview.

4. Read the News

Keeping up on the company's most recent offerings or market developments will help you prepare for your graduate job interview and serve as a terrific conversation topic!

One excellent resource for any news is Google, along with Google News.

You can probably find information by conducting a brief search that isn't available on the business's website or social media accounts.

Make sure you are up to date on any news about the company that may be mentioned during the job interview if you are aware that it can be found in a certain place, such as the Financial Times, TechUK, or FinTech Weekly.

5. Check out their competitors

Conduct competition research in addition to looking up organizations to interview with, since this will help you stay up-to-date on current market developments.

You'll comprehend the company's specialty and what makes its offering distinct.

You may utilize this information to your advantage and differentiate yourself from other candidates in your graduate job interview by understanding how to conduct research about an employer before the interview.

Know the Role
It is advisable to research the position you are looking for and its alignment with the organization's goals and framework. This entails carefully reviewing the job description to determine the essential competencies, requirements, duties, and results. It is advisable to search for comparable positions on alternative job boards or websites to gauge market demand and compensation ranges.

To gain some knowledge and guidance, you can also get in touch with people in your network or connections who currently hold or have had similar positions in the past. This will assist you in customizing your cover letter, CV, and interview responses to the position and demonstrating how you can benefit the business.

To learn more about the role, you ought to be able to use Google and other search engines.

Crafting a Compelling Resume and Portfolio
Employers may request a range of application materials from you when you apply for jobs, such as a portfolio or résumé. You can demonstrate your abilities, technical know-how, and experience with the use of resumes and portfolios. Knowing the goal and benefits of these resources can help you convince a hiring manager that you're the best person for the job.

We will explain the distinctions between a resume and a portfolio.

What is a Resume?
A resume is a formal document that applicants use to highlight their accomplishments, employment history, and educational background in hopes of being considered for a new post. Usually no more than one or two pages, it simply includes details that are specifically relevant to the job they are applying for.

In addition to their résumé, many candidates provide a personalized cover letter expressing their interest in a particular position and business. To demonstrate your fitness for the position, you can also emphasize your qualifications and skill set that align with those listed in the job description. Quantifying your accomplishments with percentages and figures is a helpful addition to both the cover letter and the CV. Such data can demonstrate the value you could provide to an organization.

What is contained in a resume?
While there are many different forms for resumes, including ones tailored to certain occupations, all resumes typically include the following information:

Professional Summary
This section provides an overview of your qualifications as a candidate. To entice a hiring manager to read the rest of the paper, you can utilize it to showcase your

accomplishments during your career, applicable abilities, and personality. When hiring, managers may browse through multiple resumes; therefore, you can stand out from the competition by creating a compelling professional summary.

Work Experience

Only include work experience that is directly related to the position you are applying for. Relevant volunteer and internship activities should also be included. Reverse chronological order is preferred by most hiring managers when listing experience.

Skills

List your hard and soft skills in this part to demonstrate your suitability for the position. Try to include the necessary abilities listed in the job description. Soft talents can include leadership, teamwork, and communication. Computer programming, graphic design, and direct sales are examples of hard skills.

What is a Portfolio?

A portfolio is an assortment of materials and data that shows off your professional experience in a graphical way. Giving examples of your greatest work to a hiring manager or potential client is a great method to demonstrate your talents and abilities. Hiring managers get to see actual samples of your work rather than just written descriptions, which helps them decide if you'd be a good fit for the role and the firm.

Various types of content, including text, images, videos, graphics, and links to websites, can usually be included in a portfolio. Portfolios are used by a variety of applicants, but they are particularly useful for creative and artistic candidates as a way to present their work. Portfolios are frequently used by writers, photographers, designers, developers, architects, and artists.

What is usually contained in a portfolio?
The presentation and format of portfolios differ. Here are some typical sections that frequently occur in portfolios to assist you in deciding what kind of information to include:

Statement of originality
Include a declaration of originality, which is a succinct text stating that the work in your portfolio is unique and private. It's also permissible to offer particular details and examples that others might not reproduce or might not copy without authorization.

Career summary
A resume that briefly summarizes your experience and qualifications is a useful tool for job seekers to introduce themselves. By highlighting specific accomplishments and providing statistics and percentages to support them, you may demonstrate your professional experience.

Statement of Philosophy
Your philosophy statement, often known as your mission statement, should include your main motivations, values,

and beliefs. You can also use this to explain what you value about your line of work.

Brief biography
You have the chance to introduce yourself to hiring managers or potential supervisors with a brief biography. You can give a brief overview of your professional trajectory, your current aspirations, and the factors that drove your decision-making. To let readers know how to reach you, you can also provide your contact information in this box.

Resumé
It's crucial to understand that a portfolio enhances a resume rather than acting as a substitute for it. By the time you get to show a recruiter your portfolio, you may have already given them your CV, but it's still helpful to have a link to it in your portfolio.

Work Samples
Since the main goal of a portfolio is to present actual examples of your work, the work sample section is the most crucial component. Try to include examples of your finest work that demonstrate all of your pertinent abilities. You can include everything from charts to articles to lesson plans, depending on your line of work. You can also discuss any honors received, constructive criticism received, or lessons discovered about particular work examples.

Portfolio vs. Resume

Even though you might know in general how a resume and a portfolio differ from one another, it could be useful to quickly review a comparison like this:

Purpose

Hiring managers want to see your resume and cover letter so they may extend an invitation for a first interview. You might provide a portfolio to hiring managers after the interview to give them a better idea of your work and qualifications.

Format

A resume is a brief document that highlights your writing abilities, employment experience, and pertinent qualities. A portfolio, on the other hand, has a greater range of content and may include images, graphs, movies, web pages, photos, and more. A portfolio can get rather large and takes some time to put together because it includes samples of your work and detailed information about your professional skills.

Requirement

While resumes are usually required for all job applications, portfolios are not always applicable. While a growing number of people outside the creative sectors are showcasing their skills through portfolios, some professions—like teaching or mechanics—may not be a good fit for this format.

How to create a professional work portfolio

To construct your work portfolio, adhere to these four steps:

1. Collect Your Materials

Assemble all the items you intend to include in your portfolio. Utilize the most up-to-date and pertinent data and examples.

These resources ought to contain:

Your Resume

Make an effort to customize your resume for certain companies or employment roles. Contact details, a professional profile, work history, education, and any applicable licenses or certifications should all be included in your resume.

A list of your skills

Look over the job description and pick the abilities you believe make you a strong candidate, along with any others that match yours. Think about classifying the skills on the list into groups like hard, soft, and self-taught.

Biographical information

A "about me" section is acceptable to have in your portfolio. It's common for interviewers to start by asking you to introduce yourself. Putting together this portfolio part will assist you in responding to this query.

Proof of any degrees, licenses or certifications

Include copies of your licenses, certificates, and educational transcripts, along with any professional development seminars you have attended, in addition to including this information on your CV. By providing this material, you establish your credibility and demonstrate your suitability for the position.

Letters of recommendation, references, testimonials or reviews

A reference contact page and client endorsements that highlight your qualifications as a professional are also acceptable. Try to find three or five individuals who are willing to provide you with constructive criticism regarding your work performance.

Work Samples

Use examples that demonstrate the variety of your abilities. Your portfolio should contain a wide range of writing examples, photos, images, project summaries, and reports, depending on your line of work. If you lack professional expertise, you might be able to use projects from voluntary work, clubs, or school.

If you have any available feedback, please include it with your samples. Add a brief synopsis, for instance, if you were promoted or achieved an exceptional grade after completing an assignment.

Military Honors and Records

Many employers are aware of the value that veterans can provide. Including military experience on your CV can demonstrate desirable behavioral traits like teamwork, leadership, a strong work ethic, and dedication, in addition to role-relevant transferable abilities.

Community service
Giving a brief overview of any volunteer work you've done that is relevant to the role or industry demonstrates your enthusiasm and commitment to the field. If you're interested in working for a nonprofit or a business that prioritizes giving back to the community, this can be quite beneficial.

Awards and accomplishments
Add more details about your accomplishments to your resume. You can go into further detail about accomplishments like employee of the month awards, academic honors, and scholarships in this section.

2. Organize your materials
Employers should be able to quickly discover information in your portfolio. Your profile, CV, and skills list should be at the top of the page. After that, order the other items in the order that you believe they should be in. Sort all of your material into categories and put them in an understandable, sensible sequence.

To help companies track your progress, you may, for instance, arrange your work samples according to when they were completed. For ease of navigation, include page numbers and create a title and table of contents page.

3. Make it visually appealing

The ability to provide visual representations of your work is one of the key advantages of building a professional portfolio. This is particularly useful for software development positions where you can showcase your original code and for UX/UI roles where you can highlight the visual enhancements you made to the user experience. For applicants pursuing careers in the arts or design, it is extremely crucial to have a visually appealing portfolio. Your portfolio should be consistently designed and organized to showcase your aesthetic, character, and working style.

Use a binder, folder, or portfolio case for hard copies of your work portfolio to make it easier to go through the pages. To help with information retrieval, tabs, section dividers, and color-coding are available. Use clear page covers to safeguard the pages.

4. Customize your portfolio

After obtaining a master copy of your portfolio, make the necessary modifications for particular job applications and interviews. Make sure that your resume and skills pages emphasize the qualifications specified in the job description.

Think about including a section on solutions. A 30/60/90 plan, which describes your work in the role for the first 30, 60, and 90 days if hired, is included in certain portfolios. You can learn more about the business and come up with suggestions on how you could support it. Employers can see that you are interested in the role and organization by looking at your 30/60/90 plan.

Tips for improving your work portfolio
1. Go Digital
An online portfolio allows you to share your work with a larger audience and is accessible whenever the audience has time to look over your whole body of work. You have a lot of choices when it comes to publishing your portfolio online. Online portfolio services are provided by numerous websites and social media networks, some of which are free. Another option is to make your website. To make your online portfolio more visually appealing, format it like a slide show and add images and infographics. Include a link to your completed web portfolio in your email signature, professional networking profiles, and résumé.

2.Make copies to share
All the essential items from your portfolio that an employer might want to maintain, such as your résumé and reference sheet, should be copied. As an alternative, print off several copies of your portfolio so you have it available for the interviewer to see whenever needed.

3.Regularly update your portfolio.
Aim to update your portfolio once a year or every few months. Regularly reviewing your portfolio will enable you to update any out-of-date content and add pertinent new material while it's still current. It's a helpful method

to assess your development and identify places for growth as well.

4.Use it as a tool to prepare for the interview process
Before an interview, you can look through your portfolio to refresh your memory on certain instances of your achievements. Portfolios are particularly useful during the interview because you may consult them for clarification on queries and to provide employers with concrete examples of your skill set. For instance, you can use the talent portion of your portfolio to help you respond appropriately if an employer asks about your biggest qualities.

Anticipating and Addressing Potential Red Flags
Have you ever had persistent concerns about an employer after an interview? You should feel fortunate to have noticed. You saw a few red flags, no doubt.

Let's imagine that when you showed up for your interview at the corporate headquarters, you were thrilled about your new employment prospect. However, the recruiting manager then made you wait an additional hour in the lobby. During your interview, he didn't make eye contact or ask about your career aspirations. Furthermore, he provided a vague response when you asked for examples of how you may apply your accounting knowledge and expertise to improve the operation and expansion of the business.

One of those gaffes during a job interview could be forgiven on its own. Nevertheless, taken as a whole, they serve as a clear reminder to gently withdraw from consideration and continue looking for new work, even if you're in a hurry to leave your current employment or need to start receiving money immediately.

Here are seven warning signs for job interviews that applicants should watch out for:

1. Valid questions get vague answers

Naturally, it is never proper for an interviewer to provide private information about a former worker. However, the recruiting manager ought to be ready to answer any questions you may have regarding the requirements for the job and provide you with some background information on the role's impact on business operations. Seek out clear responses to inquiries such as these: What will be the first obstacle the individual chosen for this position must overcome? What do you think the goal of the accounting or finance department is? What are the job's benefits and drawbacks? What information on the person to whom I would report is available to me?

1. Reasonable inquiries receive ambiguous responses

Naturally, it is never proper for an interviewer to provide private information about a former worker. However, the recruiting manager ought to be ready to answer any questions you may have regarding the requirements for the job and provide you some background information on the role's impact on business operations. Seek out clear responses to inquiries such as these: What will be the first obstacle the individual chosen for this position must overcome? What do you think the goal of the accounting or finance department is? What are the job's benefits and drawbacks? What information on the person to whom I would report is available to me?

2. The interviewer is unable to give a comprehensive description of the position

Your interviewer ought to be able to outline the duties of the position and the criteria for success, regardless of whether you're seeking the position of chief financial officer or entry-level staff accountant. If not, it will probably be challenging for you to carve yourself a distinct career path within the organization.

3. Workplace descriptions are impartial

Find out what the hiring manager enjoys most about his position at the organization. Should he be unable to respond without hesitating, it may be an indication of his discontent with his job. Ask the same inquiry of other department staff members, such as the data entry clerk and the accounting manager, if the chance presents itself during your visit. Do they appear enthusiastic about their everyday tasks? Do their efforts yield rewards? Existing prospects for promotion? Observe the "mood" in the office.

4. Short employee tenure

Employee turnover patterns may indicate a high-stress, low-morale workplace culture. You may have a toxic work environment or a negative boss situation if you find out that past employees left the company quickly and there is little indication of staff permanence.

5. The recruiting manager lacks readiness
Your potential employer should be prepared to determine whether you are a good fit for the role, just as much as you have prepared for the interview, made sure to be on time, reviewed requirements for the open position, and brought questions about the business and its objectives to the table. If the employer appears to have not read your resume or is running late for the appointment, take notice.

6. You don't find the workplace to be appealing
Be mindful of your surroundings as soon as you enter the room for your job interview. Do employees take an active role in their work, or do they just sit there like robots in their cubicles? Does your potential employer appear distant and contemptuous, or does he interact with colleagues and subordinates professionally? There's no reason to think that once you start working in the office, these problems will go away if you see them during the interview.

7. You sense that no one is paying attention to you
It's a warning sign if the recruiting manager talks the entire interview and doesn't seem to be interested in hearing what you have to say or posing meaningful inquiries regarding your professional aspirations and prior achievements. During an interview, a manager's body

language, eye contact, and general manners can all reveal whether or not he is genuinely interested and involved.

It takes initiative and planning to spot and deal with any potential red flags in your work history. You may turn possible concerns into chances to highlight your growth, resilience, and appropriateness for the position by being transparent, highlighting your experiences, and making sure they line up with the job requirements. Keep in mind that companies value sincerity, and addressing red flags early on creates a favorable and productive interview environment.

CHAPTER 3

CRAFTING IMPACTFUL RESPONSES

Your answers are the choreography in the complex dance of a job interview; they help to construct the story of your professional journey. It takes skill to craft powerful answers that communicate your experiences, credentials, and goals with confidence, clarity, and relevancy. The essential components of creating interview responses that stick are examined in this section.

The STAR Method: Structuring Your Answers for Maximum Impact
You can practice answering situational and behavioral interview questions by using the STAR interview method. The acronym, STAR stands for for **S**ituation, **T**ask, **A**ction, and **R**esult. Behavioral interview questions are used by hiring managers to assess your suitability for a position. With the aid of this technique, you can draft succinct, understandable responses based on actual situations.

How does the STAR method work?

Using the STAR approach, you may write a story that is simple to read and has a distinct conflict and resolve. The following describes each component of the technique:

Situation

Set the scene by providing background information about a particular circumstance or difficulty you overcame. Give two or three key details about related volunteer efforts, academic initiatives, or employment scenarios. Because interviewers are more interested in the activities you did and the outcomes you attained, you should spend the least amount of time on this section of your response.

Task

Explain your duty or position in the circumstances or difficulty. Speak about the objective or work that has been assigned to you. Just focus on one or two primary ideas that most clearly represent the assignment you had to finish. Like the scenario component, this section takes very little time to complete.

Action

Describe the precise steps you took to deal with the circumstances or get past the obstacle. List a handful of the most important actions you took to achieve your goal and talk about them. Use "I" to emphasize your specific contributions in your response rather than "we," even if your activities were conducted as a team. The most detailed explanation is needed for this section of your response because it primarily demonstrates your suitability for the position.

Result
What result did your actions lead you to achieve? Concentrate on two or three primary outcomes of your actions and talk about the lessons you took away, the ways you developed, and the reasons the experience has made you a more capable worker. Additionally, if at all feasible, give specific instances of how your efforts have paid off. Just a small amount of time should be spent on results discussion as opposed to action discussion.

How to prepare your STAR interview response
To help you prepare a STAR interview response for a job interview, follow these steps:

Examine the job description and the list of necessary talents, then think about the kinds of difficulties or roadblocks you would encounter in the available position. Examine the typical interview questions for conduct described in this article. It can be beneficial to prepare your responses with this in mind, even though the wording of these questions may change from interview to interview. This is because the questions usually have the same broad meaning. The interviewer might inquire about "a time you were under pressure" or "how you handled stress," for instance. In either case, they want to know how you handle stressful situations.

Jot down the different scenarios you've faced in your work that demonstrate the kinds of abilities you'll need to be successful in the available position. Assemble each example by applying the STAR technique.

Make sure each story is as clear and cohesive as possible by practicing answering questions aloud. Additionally, it will make you feel more at ease and confident when you respond to questions during an interview.

If you're just starting the job and don't have a lot of work experience, think about your volunteer activities, internships, and group projects from school. Employers might occasionally ask you to give a non-work-related example, so think about the difficulties or barriers you've surmounted in your personal life as well.

Whichever stories you choose to share, be sure to specify a setting, task, action, and outcome, as well as highlight the talents and abilities that are most pertinent to the position.

Examples of STAR interview questions
Most behavioral interviews center on a variety of work-related tasks that highlight critical thinking and problem-solving abilities, as well as scenarios that highlight leadership abilities, conflict resolution, and performance under pressure; however, the exact questions will not be disclosed to you in advance. Here is some more information about behavioral questions and some advice

on how to use the STAR approach while responding to them.

The following are some typical behavioral interview questions that you might encounter:

1. Give an instance of a challenging issue you overcame at work. In what way was this problem resolved?
2. Have you ever been forced to take a controversial stand? What was your approach to it?
3. Tell about a period when you worked under a lot of strain. What was your response?
4. Describe a mistake you have made for me. What was your approach to it?
5. Give an instance when you had to make a tough choice. How did you proceed?
6. Describe a scenario in which you recommend anything based on logic or evidence.
7. Tell me about a situation where you and your supervisor didn't agree. How did you handle it?
8. Tell us about an occasion when you had to break unpleasant news. How were you able to do that?
9. Tell me about a project you worked on in collaboration with other departments.
10. Give an instance of a failure that you experienced. What insights did the experience give you?
11. Describe a moment when you set out to accomplish a certain objective.
12. Tell me about a situation in which you had to convince someone to act.

13. Tell about a moment when you and a coworker got into a fight. What was your approach to it?
14. Have you ever needed to inspire other people? How were you able to do that?
15. When did you finish your workday early enough to do everything?

Examples of STAR method responses

Here are three instances of how to use the STAR approach to respond to common behavioral interview questions:

Give an instance of a challenging issue you overcame at work. In what way was this problem resolved?

Situation: "During prom season, I worked as a retail manager at a department store." A dress that a customer ordered online was delivered to the store. The outfit was inadvertently left out on the floor by one of my colleagues, and it was quickly bought by another customer.

Task: I was aware that to satisfy the customer and maintain the company's good name, I had to set this right.

Action: I found the identical outfit at a nearby store before calling the customer to inform her of the error. To express my gratitude for her understanding, I had it pressed and sent to her house the morning of prom along with a gift card.

Results: The client was so appreciative that she gave us multiple five-star reviews on review websites."

Tell about a period when you worked under a lot of strain. What was your response?

Situation: "One of my coworkers in my former position as an account executive departed right away after our company signed the largest customer it had ever taken on.

Task: I was given this new client in addition to the several accounts I was previously in charge of. I understood that there was a lot on the line and that we wouldn't meet our quarterly target if we lost this transaction.

Action: I started by de-stressing a little. After that, I thoroughly reviewed and reorganized my to-do list to make sure I could finish everything. As a result, I was able to give the client my full attention and gave up a few evenings and weekends to answer calls until the project was finished.

Result: The client was so pleased with my commitment that they signed a five-million-dollar annual deal with us right away.

Describe a mistake you have made for me. What was your approach to it?

Situation: "I ordered the flower arrangements for a private event thrown by a high-profile customer while I was an intern for an events firm. Sadly, I misplaced the details from another event, causing the flowers to be sent to the incorrect location across town.

Task: Since we were running out of time, I realized I had to come up with a speedy answer. I took this very seriously.

Action: I told my supervisor that I had made a mistake and explained my plan, along with the reasons for my decision to take it that way. An hour before the event, I took an early lunch break, drove to the other location, picked up the flowers, and delivered them to the right location.

Result: My supervisor was quite appreciative, and the client was unaware of my error.

Handling Difficult Questions

Your interviewer might pose questions to you in a job interview that call for more considered responses. Although difficult interview questions might differ greatly in different industries, there are a few that companies frequently use to get further information about a candidate and evaluate their abilities. You can improve your interview preparation by going over some challenging interview questions and sample responses.

Important lessons

1. Employers probe you to find out how you handle information and resolve issues.

2. Take a moment to gather your thoughts before coming up with a response to a challenging interview question. If necessary, ask clarifying questions.

3. As you respond to these questions, get ready to defend your strategy and provide supporting details.

Tough interview questions with sample answers

More challenging interview questions are asked to elicit vital details about you you that your resume might not have included. These questions aid in their evaluation of your mental processes as well as your capacity for original thought and the application of logic to various situations. Asking pointed questions might help them better understand your degree of expertise and comfort with challenging work. Think about practicing your responses to the following challenging interview questions:

What critical feedback do you most often receive?

Employers ask this question, which is akin to "What are your greatest weaknesses?" to gauge your level of self-awareness and whether you're making an effort to better yourself. Consider a real critique you've received or a flaw you know you have, together with the steps you take to overcome it, to help you answer this question. Give a succinct explanation of the criticism and your plans to address it.

Example: "I've been informed in the past that I talk over other people in meetings. Even while I enjoy working with people and getting enthused about the projects I'm working on, I also see the benefits of having a varied range of opinions and actively listening. I've made it a point to carefully listen while taking notes and to speak last while others are speaking.

Tell me about a time you overcame an obstacle.
Employers inquire about your approach to problem-solving by asking you this question. When responding to questions like these in behavioral interviews, you can apply the STAR approach. Give a succinct explanation of the circumstances, your involvement in the matter, the steps you took to address the problem and the resolution of the problem as a result. Summarize the things you discovered during the process.

Example: "During prom season, I worked as a retail manager at a department store." A dress that a buyer ordered online was delivered to the store, where it was unintentionally bought by another client. I found the identical outfit at another local location before giving the original buyer a call. In appreciation for her understanding, I had it pressed and sent a gift card to her house the morning of prom. She left us multiple five-star reviews on review sites right away.

What is your approach to managing stress?
Many occupations include stress; therefore, employers want to know that you can manage more challenging tasks and constructively handle stress while keeping a positive attitude. You might respond to this question by

providing an example that demonstrates how you usually handle stress. Employers can see from this that you can handle pressure well.

Example: I find that in difficult situations, communication is essential, even if it means talking a lot to make sure everyone is aware of the project's requirements. For instance, while I was collaborating with another team on a project, we discovered that duplicate work was being done. We accomplished a significant company goal ahead of schedule and finished the project on schedule by holding weekly standups and keeping honest lines of communication with our managers and teams.

Which managerial experiences, both good and bad, stand out to you the most?
Employers may inquire about your preferences for and dislikes of specific management styles by asking you this question. This could aid them in determining whether you would be a suitable match for a particular manager. When responding to this question, try to be as truthful and diplomatic as you can while highlighting your best qualities first.

For instance, I like cooperative managers who provide their people with the means and equipment to complete tasks as a team. My previous manager supported our brainstorming meetings with whiteboards and placed a strong emphasis on process improvement. She seemed to pay attention to my demands and assist me in getting the tools I required to accomplish my objectives. Although gifted and experienced, one of my previous bosses tended to oversee our team's work carefully and without much leeway, which limited our opportunities for growth as professionals.

What is the greatest flaw about you?
To assess your level of self-awareness, employers could inquire about your areas of weakness. They also ask it so they can find out how you're trying to enhance your abilities. Tell the truth about your biggest shortcoming and provide examples of how you're overcoming it in your response. You may then talk more about your growth attitude as a result of this.

Example: I've been working on improving my capacity to offer constructive feedback as a weakness. I know that giving comments on work or projects is helpful to my team, but in the past, I've found it difficult to do so without hurting their feelings. I've started putting my criticism in writing before approaching my coworkers to do better. This aids in my response preparation and allows me to provide a more pertinent critique.

Why are you leaving the job that you currently hold?
The reasons behind your resignation from your present job may be crucial information for companies to know. They may also ask it to make sure your departure was not due to your performance or behavior. This helps them make sure the position is a better fit for your background and skill set. While answering this question honestly, try

not to include too many excessively private or unfavorable details.

Example: Although I had a great time working for the prior company, there aren't many opportunities for me to advance in my profession anymore. My skill set is ideal for this role, and over the following few years, there will be many opportunities for me to grow in it.

Do you have any regrets so far in your professional career?
This is a question that employers might ask to find out more about your professional path and any potential weaknesses. You could talk about some of your past errors or professional shortfalls that don't impair your capacity to do the job to answer this question. Try to keep your response upbeat while you explain the lessons you've learned from your experiences.

For instance, there are moments when I regret not having known what I wanted to accomplish with my life and spending years in a field that didn't provide the kind of challenge I was looking for in a profession. I could become even more proficient in my work if I had more years to grow professionally. Nevertheless, I gained knowledge in my former employment that I would not have acquired otherwise and that I use in my current position, such as communication and time management.

What is your most notable accomplishment?

This is a question that employers may pose to gain a better understanding of your most valuable achievements. It enables them to understand your professional priorities, particularly if you have achieved several noteworthy goals. When responding, consider a current instance that somehow relates to the position. Give a brief explanation of the accomplishment, your part in it, and the reasons it means especially to you.

As an illustration, my team received a prize last year for the most creative process enhancement. It was my responsibility to set up the group so that we could discuss potential improvements to the production process. We tried three tried-and-true methods before putting the most effective one into practice. Our upgrades allowed us to quadruple our output by reducing the time to production by 20%.

Highlighting Your Achievements
Effectively communicating your accomplishments is essential to crafting meaningful answers. Showcasing your accomplishments shows your worth and skill, whether you're talking about prior initiatives, successes in former employment, or personal accomplishments.

Techniques for Expressing Accomplishments:
Quantify Impact: Whenever you can, calculate the effect that your accomplishments have had. Provide measurable metrics such as percentages, statistics, or other metrics to give concrete proof of your contributions.

Example: Within six months of implementing a new workflow, team efficiency increased by 20%.

Contextualize Challenges: Explain the difficulties or roadblocks you encountered when talking about your accomplishments. This emphasizes your resilience and problem-solving abilities.

Example: I successfully launched the project with a cross-functional team, overcoming unforeseen supply chain problems despite a tight schedule.

Emphasize Special Contributions: Explain what made your contributions special or noteworthy. This could involve creative problem-solving, showing initiative in difficult circumstances, or going above and beyond in projects.

As an illustration, I implemented a cost-cutting program that resulted in a 15% expense reduction as well as process streamlining and increased workflow efficiency.

Stress Team Collaboration: If accomplishments require cooperation, highlight your part in encouraging teamwork and attaining group success. Emphasizing cooperation abilities is especially crucial for jobs where teamwork is required.

Example: By closely working with cross-functional teams, we were able to build a customer feedback system that increased customer satisfaction by 30%.

Link Performance to Work Requirements: Make sure your accomplishments are directly related to the job specifications. This alignment demonstrates your fit for the job and makes it easier for the interviewer to see how you will contribute in the new capacity.

Example: The objectives listed in the job description are exactly aligned with my experience in increasing productivity and streamlining processes.

Employ the STAR approach: To give a thorough summary of your accomplishments, organize your comments using the STAR approach (Situation, Task, Action, Result). This technique aids in making sure your narrative is comprehensive and clear.

Situation: Describe the circumstances.
Task: Describe the precise objective or task.
Action: Describe the steps you took to complete the assignment.
Result: Draw attention to the advantageous effects or consequences of your activities.
*Example: "I found a bottleneck in our production process (location) in a prior role. It was my responsibility to optimize the procedure to boost productivity (task). I trained the team (Action) and introduced new workflows, which led to a 15% increase in overall output and a 25% decrease in production time (Result)."

Recall that the objective is to tell a gripping tale that demonstrates your influence and ability rather than merely listing accomplishments. Giving precise, quantifiable, and contextualized examples makes your accomplishments seem more credible and makes a lasting impression on the interviewer.

Tailoring Responses to Fit the Company Culture

Changing your answers to fit the corporate culture is a calculated move that shows you understand the organization's values and ethos and are flexible and aware of them. Responding in a way that aligns with the company's culture strengthens your application and highlights your potential for cultural fit.

Strategies for Tailoring Responses to Fit the Company Culture:

Research Company Values: Learn everything there is to know about the mission, values, and cultural tenets of the organization before the interview. Recognize the priorities of the organization's workspace.

Example: "After doing a lot of studies on [Company Name], I'm very intrigued by your dedication to cooperation and innovation. I started cross-functional projects in my prior position to reflect [Company Name]'s value of collaboration and innovation.

Align Personal Values: Determine which elements of the corporate culture are consistent with your professional philosophy and personal beliefs. Respond in a way that best demonstrates how your values align with those of the organization.

Example: "[Company Name]'s commitment to environmental sustainability is something I can relate to. In my prior role, I oversaw programs to lower our carbon footprint by incorporating environmentally friendly procedures into our day-to-day work."

Mirror Communication Style: Observe how the organization communicates, be it organized, informal, formal, or collaborative. Modify your answers throughout the interview to reflect this.

For instance, "I have seen that [Company Name] values open communication highly. In my experience, I've promoted open lines of communication across teams, which has enhanced cooperation and problem-solving abilities."

Emphasize Cultural Fit: Clearly state that you are interested in and in line with the company's culture. Give concrete examples from your prior experiences to demonstrate the times you flourished in a comparable cultural setting.

For instance, "Having worked in dynamic and innovative environments previously, I believe my adaptability and passion for staying at the forefront of industry trends align well with the entrepreneurial spirit I see at [Company Name]."

Display Flexibility: Show that you can adjust to a variety of cultural contexts. Give examples from your professional experience when you overcame a variety of workplace challenges or made a constructive contribution to an alteration in company culture.

As an illustration, I have worked in both startups and more established corporate organizations. I've been able to significantly contribute in a variety of cultural contexts, thanks to my versatility.

Stress either autonomy or teamwork as needed. Depending on the culture of the firm, adjust your answers to highlight personal initiative or teamwork. Strong teamwork is valued by some firms, whereas people who can operate alone are valued by others.

Example (teamwork): I have experience succeeding in cooperative settings that place a high value on team achievement. In my former position, I actively looked for chances to collaborate closely with coworkers to accomplish common objectives.

Example (autonomy): I've performed exceptionally well in positions that grant some autonomy. In my prior role, I showed that I could work independently and take the initiative to complete tasks with excellent outcomes.

You may show that you are a good fit for the firm and that you are dedicated to making a positive impact on the work environment by customizing your responses to fit the culture of the company. This connection increases your attractiveness as a candidate who not only has the required skills but also reflects the company's beliefs and culture.

CHAPTER 4

COMMON INTERVIEW QUESTIONS AND BEST RESPONSES

During a job interview, a standard series of questions is frequently asked to evaluate your qualifications, experiences, and overall fit for the position. A good interview depends on having well-thought-out answers ready for these inquiries. This section looks at some typical interview questions and offers tips for creating the most effective answers.

General Questions: Tell Me About Yourself, Why Should We Hire You?

Tell me about yourself.

This is a question that recruiters and employers alike frequently pose during first-phone interviews or recruiter screens. They also probably ask it early in the interview process. Give a brief overview of your professional experience and educational background to respond to the issue efficiently. Talk about the parts of your professional experience that are most pertinent to the position and highlight some of your proudest accomplishments.

How to Format Your Response: Start with a succinct bio, go over your work history in brief, highlight your most important experiences and accomplishments, and end by discussing how your qualifications relate to the role.

As an illustration: "Certainly! My name is [Your Name], and I have [X years] of [Your Field] experience. During my tenure at [Previous Company], I accomplished [name a significant accomplishment or duty] with success. I find the chance at [Current current company] exciting because you can use your talents for the role."

Example: "I started my career as a retail merchandising specialist in a nearby department store after receiving my associate's degree in fashion merchandising. There, I assisted in enhancing the online buying experience by organizing the weekly merchandising calendar. I oversee the growth of five fashion lines in my current position at Serial Rock Outfitters as a fashion merchandiser. I formed connections with fifteen new businesses last month, and thus far, that has helped raise revenue by more than twenty percent."

Why Should We Hire You?
Employers pose this question to learn more about your qualifications and set you apart from potential prospects. In response, describe how your qualifications, experience, and personal qualities make you the ideal candidate for the position. Before crafting your response, carefully read

the job description to ascertain the traits they are looking for in a candidate.

Highlight the unique abilities, backgrounds, and characteristics that make you stand out from the competition. Make sure your response is in line with the main job requirements and highlights how you will help the team and the firm succeed.

Example 1: "I bring a special combination of [highlight specific skills] and [emphasize relevant experiences], which is why you should hire me." I effectively [name a significant accomplishment] in my prior position at [the previous company]. My strong [name another pertinent talent] and my capacity to [emphasize quality or competency] make me an excellent fit for this role, I'm sure of it. In addition to my knowledge and expertise, I am eager to share my enthusiasm for [discuss a pertinent facet of the position or the company's goals]. I am thrilled to have the chance to significantly influence and support [Company Name's] ongoing success."

Example 2: "I think I'm a great fit for the position because of my proven office management expertise and passion for problem-solving. I made a strategy to reorganize the office supply cupboard by category while I was an office manager. We placed fewer orders that year and saved thirty percent on office supplies because they were easier to find. I can't wait to use the managerial talents I've developed over the last four years in a new position.

Why do you wish to be employed here?
This is a common question posed by employers to ensure that you have given your decision to apply for a job at their company careful thought. If you're switching to a new industry or job, this question may be especially crucial. When discussing your reasons for wanting to work for the organization, be truthful and prioritize the intrinsic benefits the position can provide over external ones like greater income and perks.

Example: "I deliberately looked for firms that are dedicated to integrity, philanthropy, and innovation when I started looking for a new position, and your company is at the top of the list. Edison Enterprises International has consistently strived to use technology to enhance the client experience because it is a forward-thinking company. This position would provide me with the perfect opportunity to apply my love of user experience to encourage innovation, which excites me."

Show off your familiarity with the business by emphasizing certain facets, such as its goals, core principles, most recent successes, or standing in the sector. Link these elements to your personal values and professional objectives.

For instance, "[Company Name]'s dedication to [such as innovation and sustainability] is impressive." Your most recent [particular accomplishment] is exactly in line with my principles, and I'm thrilled to have the chance to work for such a vibrant and progressive company."

Behavioral Questions: Describe a Challenging Situation, How You Handled Failure

Behavioral interview questions evaluate your responses and behaviors in a certain work environment or circumstance. These inquiries typically start with "Tell me about a time when..." or "Give me an example of..." and frequently have a direct connection to the main abilities or competencies needed for the position. Employers can learn more about your abilities and traits—such as communication, critical thinking, problem-solving, and customer service—through behavioral interviews. You can use the STAR approach, which consists of the following elements, to organize your responses to these questions:

Situation: Give an example of a work-related scenario that relates to the question.
What was your task in that situation? Please elaborate.
Action: Describe the steps you took to resolve the issue.
Outcome: Provide a summary of your answer.

Describe a Challenging Situation

Use the STAR approach (Situation, Task, Action, and Result) to organize your response. Give a concise account that highlights the problem, your contribution, the steps you followed, and the successful results.

Example: "We faced a significant [situation] where [explain the challenge] in a previous capacity. I had to [Task], and I went above and above by [Action]. Through these efforts, the team's performance increased and we were able to attain [Result].

A recent hire of mine, a department manager, regularly turned in reports that were not complete. They were repeatedly asked to include all the necessary data, but despite this, the reports remained incomplete and needed to be rewritten so that others could complete their tasks. I made a sample report with all the necessary information for the recruit because I was unsure if they were receiving clear information. In addition, I requested that other supervisors post a chart showing the due dates for their reports and evaluate this with their reports. As a result, not just the new employee's reports but everyone else's also increased in quality. I discovered that to achieve the intended outcomes, listening skills and clear expectation-setting are crucial.

How You Responded to Failure
This is another behavioral interview question meant to gauge your capacity for self-reflection and self-awareness. Employers use this question to gauge your ability to handle obstacles and setbacks. They assess it to gauge your fortitude and readiness to accept accountability for your deeds. Describe a particular incident of failure or challenge, emphasizing how you handled it, the lessons you took away from it, and the advantages that came from your capacity to change and advance.

Give a thorough example of a situation in which you were unable to do a task successfully, and show that you have a development mindset by emphasizing the steps you took to get better at the work.

Example: In a prior endeavor, I ran across a big obstacle where [explain the circumstances]. Even with careful planning, we ran upon unforeseen problems that caused [discuss the failure]. I responded by [describing the actions I took to resolve the matter] right away. I learned a lot from the experience about [name the learning objectives], and I made adjustments that not only fixed the immediate problem but also enhanced our procedures as a whole. My resilience was bolstered by this experience, and I now approach obstacles with a proactive perspective, prepared to adapt and learn.

Example: My team at Bright Star Shipping was given the chance to submit a bid for a contract worth millions of dollars. It was up to us to finish the sales presentation. We only had a week to prepare, but I rushed my part of the presentation and turned it in with errors and misspellings since I was focusing too much on other assignments. In addition, my team lost the contract, and I neglected to include a few crucial details in the presentations.

I discovered how crucial it is to prioritize my tasks after that event. I schedule my weekly duties in a planner and decide which more difficult items to work on during the times I know I will be most productive. I consequently gradually enhanced my time management abilities to free up more time to draft an engaging and convincing proposal for our upcoming bid."

Share an example of a career goal you had. What steps did you take to achieve it?
This question assesses your capacity to strive for your objectives. Employers also use it to gauge how you think and how motivated you are to reach your objectives. They may use it to assess your chances of advancement inside the organization. Clearly state a past career goal in your response and explain how you achieved it.

For instance, after receiving my marketing bachelor's degree, my two-year objective was to become a digital strategist for an advertising agency. Due to my lack of direct advertising expertise, I was allowed to intern at an organization where my duties included marketing insurance goods. In my spare time, I finished online courses and obtained a certification in digital advertising. I was schooled by a senior brand designer at a San Diego company last year when I was hired as an entry-level digital strategist.

Give an instance when you had to make a challenging choice. What was your approach to it?
If you're looking for a leadership role, companies might also ask you this question. It evaluates your capacity for critical and coherent thought as well as your ability to make decisions. Make use of your response to

demonstrate your sound judgment. Strive to select a choice that was critical to the expansion of the business.

As an illustration, in my prior capacity as assistant manager, I was in charge of elevating a sales team member to the sales lead role. Choosing among multiple highly qualified and self-motivated employees proved to be challenging. I decided after thoroughly examining performance evaluations and sales data. After I made the choice, I had one-on-one meetings with each contender to explain my reasoning, which helped to ease tensions and resentment before I formally announced it to the team.

It takes a careful balancing act to address how you handled failure while being resilient and keeping an eye on the lessons you learned. You can exhibit a proactive and upbeat attitude toward problems by demonstrating how you can use setbacks as chances for personal development.

Technical Questions: Job-Related and Industry-Specific Questions

Which programming language do you feel most at ease using?
To ascertain whether you are comfortable using many languages and whether you have a thorough understanding of the one they require you to use, the interviewer will likely ask you about the coding languages you are familiar with. It's crucial to include the precise coding languages you have experience with and feel

comfortable using in your response to this question. Next, indicate which particular coding language you feel most at ease using and why.

Example: Although I am proficient in several coding languages, such as SQL, Python, C++, and Visual Basic, JavaScript is the one with which I have the most practical expertise. I am most familiar with JavaScript since it was the first computer language I learned and I have worked with it on several projects over the past ten years.

How is a Storage Area Network (SAN) used?
This interview question assesses your technical proficiency concerning a particular network that you will need to understand to succeed in your position. You must explain what SAN is, what it does, and how you would utilize it in the position for which you are seeking in your response to this question.

An illustration would be a Storage Area Network or SAN. Block-level network access to storage is provided by this fast, specialized network. Applications can be made more available, performance can be improved, storage effectiveness can be increased, and data security and protection can be improved using SANs.

When is denormalizing database design appropriate?
This is a more advanced technical interview question meant to assess your ability to weigh the advantages and disadvantages of using denormalization for database

optimization. Denormalization will affect the capabilities of a database, thus it's critical to outline the benefits and drawbacks of this approach and indicate when it makes sense to apply it.

Example: To enhance a database's performance for particular queries, denormalization is a database optimization technique. When a database needs to be improved for it to satisfy the requirements of your application, denormalization can be necessary. Denormalization will, however, limit the functionality of your database, therefore before deciding to use it as an optimization strategy, be sure it is required for performance or scalability.

How do continuous integration systems function inside the automated build process?
This is a question from the interviewer to make sure you know what continuous integration technologies are and how the automated build process uses them. Give a precise definition of continuous integration in your response, followed by an explanation of how the automated build process uses it.

As an illustration, developers must integrate code into a shared repository multiple times a day as part of the continuous integration process. Every time the code is incorporated, the automatic build verifies it. This makes it possible to find errors and other issues in the codebase early on.

Interview techniques in technical terms

Here are some more pointers to help you in a technical interview make a strong impression as a candidate:

Describe your thinking.

There are definite right answers to many interview questions in technical fields. This implies that you must come up with a strategy to differentiate your response from that of the other applicants. Make an effort to differentiate yourself from the competition by explaining how you solve problems and the reasoning behind your solution.

Be familiar with various approaches to problem-solving

Technical interview questions often have multiple valid solutions. When responding to an inquiry with multiple paths to resolution, describe your approach to problem-solving and demonstrate that you are proficient in using each technique.

Ask for clarification, if needed

It's acceptable to ask the interviewer for clarification if you require more information to adequately respond to a question they pose. This will demonstrate to the interviewer your ability to recognize when more information is required and your willingness to seek clarification when necessary.

For instance: "Before I provide an answer, could you please clarify if you are referring to [specific aspect of the question] or if you would like me to address [related topic] as well?"

Elaborate on answers you don't know

It's acceptable to inform the interviewer if you are unsure about the answer to a question that comes up during a technical interview. But if this were a situation you encountered at work, you ought to go into more detail with your response and describe how you would go about obtaining the information needed to provide an answer. This will demonstrate to the interviewer your capacity to look up information when you don't know how to perform things.

Be ready to demonstrate your abilities.

A common component of technical interviews is the demonstration of your abilities through a series of brainteasers, remote coding projects, or whiteboard coding tasks. It is crucial to be ready for at least one brainteaser question or whiteboard challenge during your first technical interview, even if this phase usually happens during the second or third one. It's crucial to keep in mind that when answering these questions, you should justify your thinking and the procedures you took to arrive at your conclusion.

Case Study Questions: Analyzing and Solving Real-world Scenarios

Case study questions evaluate your capacity for critical thought, scenario analysis, and solution formulation. You show the interviewer that you have strategic thinking and problem-solving abilities by taking a thorough approach to the case study, taking into account different viewpoints, and offering well-supported solutions.

Best Response Strategy:
Recognize the issue: Start with being well-versed in the case study's specifics. If necessary, seek clarification and make sure you understand the situation, the difficulties, and the goals.

Example: Let me make a few clarifications before moving on to the answer. Could you elaborate on [particular case study feature] and verify whether [particular assumption] is true?

Describe Your Method: Describe an organized method for examining and resolving the situation. Divide the issue into its essential parts, find pertinent information, and describe the process you would follow to find a solution.

Example: I would use a methodical approach to this case study. I would start by defining the issue and pointing out important components, such [list pertinent components]. After that, I would compile pertinent data and analyze to identify trends and patterns. Lastly, I would create an all-encompassing solution that considers [certain factors].

Examine Different Viewpoints: Show that you can take into account different viewpoints and variables that could affect the issue. Talk about possible difficulties, dangers, and other options, demonstrating a comprehensive approach to problem-solving.

Example: It's crucial to take into account a variety of viewpoints when examining this case. For example, we ought to investigate potential issues like [name an issue], weigh the risks involved, and consider other options. By taking into account a variety of aspects, we can provide a solid and knowledgeable solution.

Quantify and Qualify Your Solutions: Include both quantitative and qualitative information in your solution proposals. Provide evidence to back up your suggestions and illustrate how your suggested fixes would affect society as a whole.

Example: Regarding remedies, I would suggest [particular remedy]. There is data to support this technique that shows [quantify the impact]. Furthermore, qualitatively speaking, this solution is in line with [discuss qualitative elements like business values or industry best practices].

Conclusion and Next Steps: Summarize your main conclusions, offer your suggested fixes, and indicate the next course of action. Exude confidence in your strategy's efficacy.

Example: In conclusion, I suggest putting [certain solutions] into practice to deal with the issues that were found. This is based on the analysis. The following actions would entail [specify the next steps or actions], guaranteeing a seamless and successful implementation procedure.

CHAPTER 5

MASTERING NON-VERBAL COMMUNICATION

In job interviews, nonverbal communication is important since it affects the interviewer's perception of you. Gaining proficiency in non-verbal indicators like gestures, body language, and facial expressions is essential for projecting professionalism, assurance, and positive engagement. This section examines important facets of nonverbal communication and offers tips for becoming proficient in these areas when doing interviews.

THE POWER OF BODY LANGUAGE: BUILDING CONFIDENCE AND RAPPORT

Many people find that job interviews are nerve-racking, but it's important to remember the significance of body language. Interviewers can be greatly influenced by nonverbal clues, which can shape their opinion of your professionalism, self-assurance, and fit for the position. To help you project the appropriate image and land the job you want, this article will examine the importance of body language during interviews and offer helpful recommendations.

The importance of body language

One way that you can communicate nonverbally is through your body language, which conveys your goals, attitudes, and feelings. According to research, it can make up as much as 55% of the message you convey to other people; the remaining 25% comes from your words and voice. During a job interview, your body language can support or contradict your spoken words, thus affecting the interviewer's perception of your abilities, character, and suitability for the position.

How to appear confident

Candidates with confidence, which displays self-belief and the capacity to take on difficulties and responsibilities, are frequently sought after by employers. When it comes to your body language, keep your posture straight and open. Steer clear of hunching your shoulders, crossing your arms, and slouching. Make aggressive, upbeat gestures, but make sure they stay within your body's boundaries. Refrain from fiddling with your hair, caressing your face, or fidgeting. Making eye contact with the interviewer while you speak and listen is a sign of decency, focus, and honesty. However, you should occasionally break eye contact to prevent appearing uncomfortable. Show interest by glancing at various areas of the interviewer's face, but avoid staring or blinking excessively.

How to show interest

Companies frequently want applicants who exhibit excitement for the position, business, and sector. When you smile and nod in response to questions, greet the interviewer, or hear anything you find interesting, you are demonstrating your interest through your body language. Furthermore, bend your head and lean forward to convey interest and involvement. Finally, you can build rapport and trust by mimicking the body language of the interviewer. But it should be done organically and quietly; for instance, you can cross your legs after a few seconds, but not exactly like the interviewer.

How to stay away from errors

Some body language patterns can make or break your chances of landing the job, even if you have the best of intentions. Avoid lying or overstating things in an interview to make sure it goes well because the interviewer can tell if you are being dishonest or inconsistent. Furthermore, take care not to come across as bored or uninterested, as this could irritate the interviewer and give you a less-than-professional impression. Finally, avoid acting disrespectfully or rudely; these actions might harm your reputation and give the impression that you are conceited or immature. When in doubt, remain focused and excited during the interview, engage in active listening, respect the views of others, and express gratitude to the interviewer for their time. In the end, be truthful and reasonable about your abilities, accomplishments, and experience while supplying proof to back up your statements.

Strategies for positive body language:
Keep Your Posture Correct: With your shoulders back, sit or stand upright. Proper posture exudes professionalism and confidence.

Eye Contact: Keep your eyes open naturally and consistently. It conveys honesty and attentiveness.

Shake hands firmly and confidently, matching the other person's grasp strength. Since a handshake is frequently the beginning of a physical encounter, make it memorable.

Pay attention to the way you display your facial emotions. Express enthusiasm or understanding with proper expressions and a natural smile.

Gestures: Make deliberate motions to highlight ideas, but refrain from making unnecessarily large or distracting movements. When utilized carefully, gestures can improve communication.

Mirroring: To build rapport, softly mimic the interviewer's body language. Keep your tempo and vigor within reasonable limitations.

Reduce Your Fidgeting: Try not to fidget too much by shaking your leg or tapping your fingers. It could elicit anxiety and be distracting.

Dressing for Success: Making A Positive First Impression

1.Focus on who you are rather than what you're wearing. It's too loud if your attire overwhelms your personality! The details of this will be elucidated in the items that follow. For the time being, keep in mind that your attire should appear polished but not as though you're getting ready to walk a runway. You shouldn't overly display your sense of style during an interview (unless the employer works in that field!). The primary purpose of an interview is to facilitate communication between a prospective employee and the employer. Remain mindful of the discussion's objective and dress comfortably while also projecting professionalism.

2. Adhere to the guidelines—formal isn't always preferable!

When you think about attire appropriate for an interview, you may picture a formal dress or a suit and tie. However, did you know that not all interviewers require you to wear professional attire? Pay close attention to the interview guidelines. Some people could ask you to dress in polo shirts or in the same clothes you would if you were going to work (e.g., scrubs, manual labor gear). If in doubt, you can always get in touch with HR to find out what kind of attire is appropriate for your next interview. Having said that, the majority of interviewers will be expecting you to wear business attire.

3. Make sure it Fits!

Your first impression will be affected if your blazer, jacket, or pants are too big or too tiny, even if you're wearing the most professional outfit you own. Try on those formal attire items in your closet before the day of the interview if you haven't worn them in a few years! Unfitting clothes will not only make you look bad, but it will also be uncomfortable and restrict your movement. It is not appropriate to fiddle with your attire during the interview. Make sure you dress professionally but comfortably so that your entire attention is on the interviewer.

4. Remove wrinkles

Do your slacks have noticeable wrinkles in them? Is your button-down shirt rumpled? Make sure your clothing is wrinkle-free the day you wear it for a polished first impression. Get out your steamer or iron, or use the wrinkle-care option on your machine to tumble dry your garments. If you don't have access to the aforementioned techniques, you can still take your garments to the dry cleaners. Make sure your clothing is nice and properly ironed, no matter what you do.

5. Wear slacks rather than jeans

Even though they may be cozy, jeans are too informal for a job interview (unless the instructions specifically state otherwise!). This is especially true if your jeans are ripped. Stick to slacks and other formal, well-pressed pants, or a formal skirt or dress, in place of jeans.

6. Steer clear of strong scents

however wearing perfume or cologne may seem professional, so it's best to avoid doing so (however deodorant is a huge yes, always!). People's sensitivity to specific odors varies (some even develop allergies!). During the interview, you don't want to give your interviewer a severe case of allergies. Recall that you want the interviewer to focus on your presentation and words rather than your scent.

7. Don't Overdo the Jewelry

Similar to scent or perfume, jewelry can divert attention. Earrings and necklaces can detract from the way you portray yourself overall, while bracelets and rings can clank on the table. Consider the interviewer's work culture while choosing your jewelry. Simple, elegant jewelry, like a watch or a pair of tiny earrings, is always a good choice.

8.Formal and conservative is a reliable option.
The most neutral option for an interview is simple, plain, conservative clothing, yet much depends on the culture of the workplace. You look more professional the less skin you are exposing. That means no ripped clothes, open collars, plunging necklines, shorts, flip-flops, or bare midriffs. Steer clear of ballcaps, t-shirts, logos, and brand names. Bright colors can be quite eye-catching, but pay attention to patterns. Once more, you want everyone to notice you, not what you're wearing!

9. To find the appropriate style, review the company culture and give HR a call.

Like how you might dress differently for a formal dinner or wedding than for Disney or the beach, every firm you interview with will have its own culture and style of expression. One technique to demonstrate that you'll blend in with the other workers and the office culture is through your attire. Check out the corporate website (or, if convenient and suitable, stop by the firm premises). What clothes do the staff members wear? You can also give HR a call and inquire about suitable interview dress if you're not sure.

Managing Nervousness And Anxiety: Tips For Staying Calm And Collected

The body's natural reaction to perceived threats, both real and imagined, is the nerve system. The body begins preparing to fight or run when the stress response is triggered. This can include physical reactions including pale or flushed skin, clamminess, shaking, and rapid breathing or heartbeat.

These are automatic reactions that can be useful in perilous situations but also cause anxiety in less dangerous situations. Thankfully, there are several methods and strategies you can attempt to reduce your interview anxiety.

Tips for reducing anxiety before the interview

The following five suggestions will help you de-stress before a job interview:

1. Get ready
Fear of the unknown is a major cause of interview anxiety. Although we can never be sure what questions we will be asked, being ready for the most frequent ones will help ease your anxiety. Do some research on the business, rehearse your answers to frequently asked interview questions, conduct a practice interview with a buddy, and prepare your notes and CV before the interview.

Jot down any queries you may have, specific details about yourself that you would like the employer to be aware of, and any other important information you would like to bring up or recall. When you feel like your mind is going blank during the interview, it's a terrific idea to be able to swiftly consult your notes.

Find out as much as you can about the person conducting the interview. Are they the immediate supervisor or hiring manager for this position? Are you meeting with a group of people or just one person? You'll feel more at ease and ease if you know what to anticipate.

2. Arrange your schedule to fit the interview in.
If you follow your schedule and whatever plans you may have, your day will go more smoothly. If at all feasible, schedule your job interview for the morning to avoid being anxious and waiting all day.

Make sure you get enough sleep the night before to ensure that you are awake. To ensure you have something enjoyable to look forward to following the interview, schedule a fun or interesting excursion.

3. Have your morning meal.
To ensure you have the energy you need for your interview, eat a healthy breakfast. Being hungry can make you feel more anxious and stressed. To improve your mood, pick one of your favorite dishes.

4. Speak with a friend or relative
Speaking with a happy friend or relative can make you feel a lot more confident. Receiving compliments from a loved one might reduce anxiety because it's simpler to listen to someone else speak positively than to speak yourself.

5. Take a rest.
Exercising outside releases feel-good neurochemicals and is beneficial to mental health. To help you decompress, try taking a fifteen-minute break before your job interview or taking a five-minute walk before entering the facility.

Strategy to Overcome Anxiety in the Interview Room
1. Make use of the STOP technique

One mental strategy to assist you get through stressful times is the STOP approach. The steps involved in this method are:

Stop whatever you're doing and concentrate on what you're thinking.
Take a deep breath as many times as necessary.
Observe the activities taking place within your body. Keep an eye on your feelings, the things that are going through your head, and the reasons behind them.
Proceed to apply what you have observed to the next steps you take.

The STOP technique aims to help you slow down and become conscious of your actions and feelings in the present. It enables you to keep in mind that you are in charge of your ideas and behaviors.

2. Pay attention to your breathing and hold off on speaking.
Pay attention to your breathing as much as you can. This will prevent your thoughts from straying and your emotions from getting out of control. Take a breath and wait for a moment before you speak. Being aware of your breathing helps you stay collected, and giving yourself time to gather your thoughts and respond thoughtfully before speaking helps you do so.

3. Keep in mind that you are conversing.
Stress can also be reduced by changing the way you perceive interviews. Remember that a job interview is a

discussion, not a question. Not only are they attempting to ascertain whether you are the most qualified candidate for the job, but this is also your opportunity to ascertain whether the role and the organization are a suitable match for you.

Being inquisitive and prepared with questions will assist in reducing feelings of intimidation and establish a more equitable power dynamic.

4. Be assured

Engage in active listening during the interview by using nonverbal clues like smiling and nodding. You can also fool your mind into thinking you're pleased by smiling, which will help you unwind a little more.

It takes self-awareness and proactive tactics to manage anxiety and nervousness, which is a continuous process. You can do interviews with poise and give potential employers your best self by accepting normalcy, being well-prepared, using relaxation techniques, keeping a good self-talk pattern, and concentrating on the topic at hand.

CHAPTER 6

NAVIGATING SPECIALIZED INTERVIEWS

This chapter explores the subtleties of specialized interviews and offers customized advice for situations where typical interview procedures are not followed. Technical reviews, case study assessments, and industry-specific conversations are examples of specialized interviews. This post will teach you some useful preparation techniques for both phone and video interviews, which will help you stand out from the competition and leave a good impression.

Phone And Video Interviews: Overcoming The Challenges
Employers are increasingly using video and phone interviews to examine candidates remotely. They do, however, also provide some particular difficulties that call for cautious planning.

Choose a suitable location
Selecting a good setting free from background noise, interruptions, and distractions is one of the first steps in preparing for a phone or video interview. The ideal

location for you to sit should be somewhere calm, well-lit, and welcoming with a neutral or business backdrop. To prevent any technical issues during the interview, you should also test your phone or other video equipment, including your internet connection, microphone, and camera.

Research the company and the role
Investigating the business and the position you're seeking is a crucial part of being ready for both phone and video interviews. The company's goals, beliefs, culture, goods, and services, as well as the particular demands, challenges, and expectations of the position, should all be thoroughly researched. This will enable you to prepare some pertinent questions for the interviewer and customize your responses to demonstrate how you suit the role and the organization.

Practice your answers and your delivery
Practice your responses and delivery as a third crucial stage in preparing for phone and video interviews. Examine the most typical interview questions and prepare succinct, targeted, and pertinent responses that showcase your abilities, accomplishments, and character. To project professionalism, excitement, and confidence, you should also practice your delivery, including tone, speed, volume, and body language. You can rehearse by filming yourself, having a friend or relative conduct a fictitious interview with you, or by utilizing online resources or applications that offer feedback.

Put on a professional and appropriate outfit.

Getting ready for a phone or video interview involves four essential steps: dressing professionally and appropriately. You should still dress as though you are meeting the interviewer in person even though you aren't. You should wear something appropriate for the interview's level of formality as well as the company's dress code and culture. Additionally, anything that is overly vivid, gaudy, or eye-catching—such as jewelry, accessories, or patterns—should be avoided. A tidy, well-groomed appearance that conveys your regard and enthusiasm for the role should be your goal.

Group Interviews: Standing Out In A Collaborative Setting

The idea of group interviews might be intimidating for many job seekers. They offer a distinct set of difficulties, such as standing out from the plethora of applicants and working cooperatively with possible colleagues. However, you may convert these difficulties into opportunities if you comprehend the dynamics of group interviews and prepare appropriately. Let's look at some strategies for making an impact and sticking out in a group interview.

Understand The Purpose Of Group Interviews

Employers can evaluate several candidates' interpersonal skills, leadership potential, and team dynamics in a single session by using group interviews, which are a useful tool. Understanding this goal will help you match your behavior to what the interviewers are looking for, which is the capacity to contribute to a team successfully while also making an impression as an individual.

Do your homework
Researching the organization, its principles, and its culture will provide you with a strong basis. With this knowledge, you'll be able to explain how your qualifications and experience meet the needs of the business and make thoughtful comments in group discussions.

Create A Powerful First Impression
In a group context, first impressions are especially important. Present yourself properly, be punctual, and provide a firm handshake and confident smile to everyone you meet. An upbeat, enthusiastic manner can establish the tone and set you out right away.

Display Your Teamwork Capabilities
Prove at the interview that you can collaborate successfully with others. Show consideration, pay close attention, and reply intelligently to the remarks made by other contenders. Acknowledge and expand on well-thought-out suggestions to demonstrate your cooperative attitude.

Demonstrate Your Leadership Skills
Demonstrating your leadership potential is another way to stand out in a group interview. This isn't about taking over the conversation; rather, it's about directing it in a constructive direction, asking the more reserved

members to contribute, or when necessary, providing a summary of the group's opinions.

Speak With Confidence and Clarity
When it's your moment to talk, make sure you're confident, clear, and concise. Provide direct answers to inquiries and express your ideas clearly. Being confident is infectious and can assist you in politely demanding attention.

Talk Back To The Interviewers
Engage with the interviewers as well; it's important to have nice interactions with the other candidates. Make sure to keep eye contact, use their name, and pose meaningful inquiries. Be interested in what they have to say, and answer appropriately.

Remain Calm and Positive
In a group interview, keeping a positive outlook in the face of difficulty can help you stand out. Remain calm, control your emotions, and approach arguments or differences of opinion in a professional manner.

Mastering the Group Interview
Although they could appear scary, group interviews are a great way to demonstrate your leadership and collaborative abilities. You may make a lasting impression on peers and potential employers during a group interview by being well-prepared and using these tactics. Recall that the objective is to demonstrate your capacity

to positively impact the team and the organization, not merely to outperform the competition. We at Employment Solutions are here to guide you through these difficulties and put you on the road to achievement.

In a group interview, you might be asked the following kinds of questions:

1. Who would you hire and why, given your knowledge of the other applicants in this room?
Interviewers pose this question to find out if you have good decision-making abilities and have been observing other people's responses. As the other applicants identify themselves and talk about their backgrounds and experiences, pay attention. This might help you exhibit your listening skills as well as your comprehension of the job's needs.

Example response: I propose that Peter be appointed to the role of marketing strategist. He sounds comfortable with a range of marketing automation software solutions in addition to having a wealth of agency and in-house experience.

2. How would you respond if you witnessed a coworker robbing a store?
Interviewers may assess your expertise in handling challenging situations in front of a group by asking ethical questions. They'll also hear about your encounters with particular industry standards for how to handle typical situations. Make sure you are aware of the routes you

should use to address business-related inquiries before responding to questions of this nature.

Example response: By industry norms, I would file a loss prevention report and approach my HR manager immediately, allowing them to handle it using their established procedures.

3. What makes you think you're the best candidate for this job?
This is a question that interviewers use to find out why you think you are different from the other applicants and to test your level of self-awareness. This is an excellent chance to highlight important abilities and achievements that others might not have brought up.

Example response: With over five years of experience as a customer service representative, two years of leadership experience, and fluency in both Spanish and English, I feel I'm a good fit for the customer service manager role. These skills enable me to interact with a wider range of clients.

4. What abilities do you think are most critical to this role's success?
This question is used by interviewers to learn more about your comprehension of the role and how you might use your abilities to succeed.

Example response: I think that problem-solving and empathy are the two most important abilities for someone hoping to succeed as an account manager. While problem-solving demonstrates your ability to address their demands, empathy enables you to establish a connection with the client and win their trust.

6.3 Interviews in the Second and Third Rounds: Building on Prior Success

At this point, some career advisers estimate your odds of landing the job at 1 in 4, while others put it as high as 50%. Even though the field is getting smaller, it's still critical to set yourself apart and make an impression on potential employers. The following are some things to do and avoid to ace your follow-up or last interview:

The Dos

Be Prepared
Make sure you know exactly where the interview is being held and how long it will take by making a trial run to the place.
Please keep in mind these three words: More, More, More. A second interview will probably involve more preparation, more people, more questions, more intensity, more pressure, and a higher chance of getting the job than the first.

Even more than you did for the first interview, conduct research. Before the initial interview, you most likely did some research on the business. It's time to investigate that research even more. Speak with corporate insiders: According to some experts, this is one of the most effective strategies to get ready for a follow-up interview. Seek out former students from your university or members of your sorority or fraternity who are employed by the company if you are a college student. Additionally, make sure you read trade journals to stay current on advancements in your sector or field.

Make an effort to ascertain in advance the precise nature of the agenda and the people you will be interviewing. When the interview is scheduled, ask the person you've been in contact with for more information if you haven't given it.

Make sure you have a restful night's sleep the night before this possibly demanding day. Additionally, search for chances to reenergize oneself on the day of the interview. During pauses in the activity, refresh yourself by taking a quick stroll or sprinkling some water on your face. If there isn't a lunch break, bring a little food that fits in your pocket or purse. Sustain your vigor, self-assurance, and excitement.

What to Anticipate
If you're asked to lunch with representatives of your potential company, be sure you know the proper protocol for business meals.

Please note that you may be required to take psychometric tests covering topics including personality, IQ, and talents. Other than getting a good night's sleep, there isn't much you can do to get ready for them.

You should anticipate receiving both new and some of the same questions that you were asked during the initial interview. Questions during the second interview might focus more on your personality, a particular technical talent, or both. Don't worry about repeating yourself—you will! Just make sure your answers are relevant and consistent for every person you meet with.

Even if they weren't posed at the first interview, do be prepared for behavioral questions, which are frequently asked during follow-up interviews.

Assessment
Pay attention to hints that reveal the core qualities the employer looks for in a new worker and that pertain to the requirements, worries, challenges, and issues you would be expected to manage.

Make sure you have a ton of questions ready to ask. In the second interview, you'll probably have more time to ask questions and be expected to ask more in-depth questions than you did in the first.

Final Words of Advice
If you are not contacted with an offer, do inquire about the next steps in the procedure. When a decision is made, what will be the process for informing you?

Make an effort to get the business cards from every person you encounter during the second interview. In the unlikely event that you are unable to obtain a card from someone, always have a little notepad on hand to jot down names.

The Don'ts:
Be Prepared
Don't forget to evaluate how you performed in the initial interview. Make a note of any queries or circumstances that gave you trouble, then prepare an improved response for those instances at the follow-up interview. Come up with a list of fresh successes, fresh case studies, and fresh proof of your depth of knowledge of the company.

Don't skimp on the clothing for the interview. In most cases, a second interview does not indicate a more relaxed one.

Anticipation
If the interviewer brings up pay and perks, don't be shocked. You may be questioned about your readiness to move and travel, so prepare your answers. Don't discuss salaries until you have an offer, please. Refrain from responding right away if the employer extends an offer. Give yourself a few days to consider it.

If some of the people you meet aren't very skilled interviewers, don't be astonished by it. Although first interviewers are frequently managers with interviewing experience, some of the persons you may speak with during the second interview may not have interviewing experience.

If there are other individuals in the room during your interview, don't be alarmed. Make eye contact with everyone in the room or on the panel while you answer a question, not just the one who posted it.

Assessment

It might make for a long day if the second interview turns out to be a series of interviews, conducted in both individual and group/panel settings. Interviews can be conducted with department heads, managers, senior executives, and potential team members. In addition, you might be taken out to lunch and given a tour of the office.

Remember to have conversations with people outside of the folks you are interviewing. Engaging in light conversation with the front desk agent and potential coworkers will help you gauge your level of interest in the work environment and leave a good impression.

Closing

Remember to take notes during and immediately following the interview. This is useful for writing thank-you messages, assessing how the interviews went, and deciding whether you are interested in the position or business.

Remember to thank every person you meet by email or note. You heard correctly—every single one. Are you not happy that you gathered those emails and business cards? Even though you can write the same general note to each person, try including a personal note that you discussed with them.

Candidates can confidently navigate advanced rounds and make a lasting positive impression on potential employers by strategically reflecting on previous rounds, building on established rapport, addressing deeper skill assessments, emphasizing cultural fit, handling multiple interviewers adeptly, posing probing questions, managing salary discussions, and following up effectively.

CHAPTER 7

HANDLING CURVEBALLS: UNCOMMON INTERVIEW SCENARIOS

This chapter covers unusual interview scenarios and offers techniques for handling curveballs with grace and flexibility, preparing candidates for the unexpected. To gauge applicants' adaptability, interviewers may pose unusual questions or put them in unusual settings. This chapter gives readers the tools they need to deal with unforeseen obstacles and make a good first impression.

7.1 Unorthodox Questions: Thinking on Your Feet

We'll look at the logic behind odd interview questions and provide tips on how to be ready for them. We'll also explore the psychology of the pizza topping question and how your response can provide insight into your character and aptitude for the position.

Asking unconventional interview questions might help companies gauge a candidate's inventiveness and personality. Numerous kinds of questions can be asked during a job interview. To present yourself and your skills in the best possible light, it's critical to be ready for any kind of question. Knowing the various kinds of interview questions can help you feel prepared and confident when you go into your next interview to make an impression on your prospective employer.

Thinking on your Feet: Unveiling the Purpose Behind Interviewers' Unconventional Questions

1.To assess your response to unforeseen circumstances: Asking unusual questions can help you assess your ability to handle change, which is a valuable skill in many fields.

2.To evaluate your capacity for creativity and problem-solving: Asking odd questions can help the interviewer gauge your capacity to think creatively and outside the box if the position requires it.

3.To distinguish amongst candidates: Interviewers may pose atypical questions to test candidates' ability to think quickly and generate original responses, which can help them stand out from the crowd.

.4To evaluate your cultural fit and personality: Some odd inquiries may be meant to gauge your personality and suitability for the company's culture.

5.To spice things up: When interviewing multiple candidates for the same position, interviewers may choose to use out-of-the-ordinary questions to make the conversation lively and memorable.

Strategies that can help them increase their chances of success

Remain composed and at ease: Remind yourself that the interviewer is interested in learning about your personality and cognitive process. Breathe deeply and unwind.

Pay close attention: Before responding, make sure you comprehend the question completely, seek clarification if necessary, and organize your thoughts.

Be sincere and truthful: While considering the job criteria and corporate culture, give a sincere response.

Display your individuality: Make the most of this chance to highlight your special talents and attributes.

Think imaginatively and outside the box: Don't be scared to use your imagination or adopt an alternative strategy.

Employ narratives and examples: Provide pertinent anecdotes and examples to support your answers.

Practice ahead of time: You might feel more at ease and confident during the real interview by practicing beforehand.

You need to be prepared for the following queries that they might pose:

1. Explain your approach to leadership.
2. Tell me about a challenging client you worked with.
3. Tell me about an instance where you had to convince someone.

4. Tell me about an instance where you didn't agree with someone.

5. Tell me about a time you set and accomplished a goal for yourself.

6. Tell me about an instance where you exceeded people's expectations.

Let's examine the response to the questions. The interviewer is looking for a few things when you are asked to "think on your feet," such as:

- Capable of handling stress and acting fast

- Are you capable of using critical thinking to problem-solving?

- Able to speak succinctly and effectively in a meeting or under pressure

Advice: You should be prepared to give a few salient ideas and examples to respond to this question effectively. These have to be focused on your skills and the reasons you are the most qualified applicant for the position. As an illustration:

My background in X and Y makes me a strong candidate for this role. When X occurred in my prior employment, I had to react quickly. I was able to think of a solution and put it into action very fast, leading to Y. This proved that I could work under pressure and think of original solutions.

I believe that my experience in Z further qualifies me for this position. I had to react quickly in my prior work when X occurred. I was able to think of a solution and put it into action very fast, leading to Y. This proved that I could work under pressure and think of original solutions.

I think my background and quick thinking make me the most qualified applicant for this position.

Here's another piece of advice: after responding to the question, it's critical to pose a few of your own. This demonstrates your enthusiasm for the role, your familiarity with the business, and your research skills. As an illustration:

I would need further information on the team I will be working with.

What are the principal obstacles that this department must overcome?

What is the business's X strategy?

You can demonstrate your interest and engagement in the role by posing questions. This will help you stand out from the other applicants and leave a positive impression on the interviewer. Additionally, don't forget to check them out on LinkedIn. You might discover that you two share hobbies or interests, which always helps to "break the ice!"

Dealing with Silence and Unexpected Interruptions

After completing your sentence, there was stillness. And then comes the dreaded awkward pause. With your hands, what do you do? Do you have something to say?

Likely, a pause that seems awkward to you may not be awkward to the person conducting the interview. He or she can formulate the next question or mentally and physically take notes. It's quite normal to be silent at times, so wait to speak again until you've given them a chance to absorb what you just said.

Avoid simply babbling to fill the void in the conversation since this could throw off the hiring manager's train of thinking. What if, instead, he or she is simply pausing to acknowledge in their mind how amazing you are?

Here are some pointers to help you appreciate the significance of the quiet.

During an interview, as a recruiter, a lot of thoughts cross my mind. I have the primary responsibility of taking as many notes as I can. Since I need to provide the hiring manager with accurate information, I don't want to miss anything the candidate says. There are moments when I have to stop and process this. Having said that, I do occasionally employ silence as a test to gauge a candidate's reaction to pressure. Similar to this, hiring managers evaluate a candidate's comfort level and emotional intelligence through silence. Allow the uncomfortable quiet to pass to emerge victorious. Be composed. Say, "Is there anything else I can fill in on that point?" after counting slowly to five. Use this time to gather your thoughts for the remainder of the talk and to think back on your responses.

Come prepared.
Long before you enter the room and shake the interviewer's hand, your war plan begins. Get comfortable responding to open-ended questions by practicing your responses to frequently asked questions with your friends. Organize each argument so that it relates to your studies, your work, or the reason you are interested in this specific career. I suggest utilizing the STAR format to ensure that every aspect has been covered:

Situation: What was the background or context?
Task: Specifically, what had to be done?
Action: How did you go about achieving the desired outcome?
Result : How did it go overall in terms of outcome and reception?

You won't feel the need to continue speaking only to fill the void if you are confident that you have covered every topic you have practiced.

Know your audience.
The employment procedure probably involves several interviews for you. Usually, it begins with a chat with a human resources representative or recruiter. This could

be your chance to take the lead in the conversation a little bit more. You will want to be a little more submissive if and when you advance to the following round of the application process and meet with the hiring manager. That is not to say that you shouldn't have room to ask questions; on the contrary, you should. Nevertheless, you can't control the situation, so when the quiet does occur, let it pass so the hiring manager can go on to the next item on their list.

Avoid digressing.
I've had applicants talk so much that their words cease making sense, and I know it's nerves. One interviewee—which makes sense—began by talking about her current position before going into detail on why she doesn't get along with a certain coworker. That's not good. A candidate typically loses focus and begins attempting to make incorrect connections when they speak endlessly. I once asked a job candidate, for instance, to provide me with an example of a moment when he received comments on his work and how he handled it. He got off to a good start by mentioning a particular project, but he soon veered off-topic and gave a detailed analysis of his manager's challenging nature. He not only did not respond to the query posed, but he also gave the impression that he was not the source of the issue.

There is still hope if you find yourself taking this path. You did not mess up the interview. Simply accept my rambling apology and request to "start over." It's acceptable to acknowledge when an interview doesn't go as planned. Sincerity is the most valued quality by recruiters.

Addressing Uncomfortable Topics: Gaps in Employment, Salary Expectations and Gaps in Employment
First of all, you should be aware that you are not the only one with a lapse in your work history. The vast majority of people have experienced unemployment at some point in their working-age life, according to the Bureau of Labor Statistics.

Tips on how to address gaps in your work history in an interview.
Employment gaps are times in your professional career when you were not employed in a formal capacity, either by choice or by necessity. A gap in employment should be recognized if it exceeds six months. If you don't include an explanation for your employment gap and the experience you acquired during that period, employment gaps on your resume may raise red flags.

You could have experienced a gap in employment due to the following reasons:

Attended to an ill relative
Stayed at home to take care of your kid or kids
Had problems with their health or medication
Pursued professional training or additional education;
Traveled or relocated
Were fired or laid off

Actively looked for a new position but was unable to find one that fit

How to explain employment gaps
During an interview, there are a few simple rules to follow while explaining work gaps:

1. Be ready to discuss it.
You won't necessarily be unable to get through the interview process if your CV has a gap. However, employers to come will demand an explanation. Spend some time in advance figuring out how to bridge the gap in a way that conveys assurance and optimism.

2. Have integrity
You want to tell the facts without providing needless details. You may start your response with something like this: I [reason you were not employed]. That's when you [did what you did in the interim]. During that time, going back to work was my primary priority, and I'm prepared to do so today.

The following are some possible causes of your employment gap, along with suggestions for how to customize the template to fit your circumstances:

If you quit your job to take care of someone else, I was my family's primary caregiver for a while. I was able to support my family at that time, but I was always aware that I wanted to go back to work. Right now, I'm prepared to carry that out.

If you lost your job

My employment was removed as a result of reorganization at my previous employer. It was, to be honest, a trying moment. However, I departed with the knowledge that I had gained valuable skills there and solidified my bonds with my supervisors and coworkers. I'm excited about the chance to use those experiences in my upcoming position.

If you were let go

I had different expectations from the firm. As I think back on that incident, I see some things I could have done differently. I feel like I've learned a lot, and I can't wait to apply that maturity to my future position.

If I took time off for personal reasons, I was able to focus on myself by taking a break from work. It was a period that equipped me to face new difficulties. The prospects that lay ahead, like this job, have me giddy with anticipation.

3. Close the distance

You don't have to elaborate on the reasons behind your job gap, but you should describe in depth what you did throughout that period.

Talk about what you read to stay current on industry news, how you kept in contact with colleagues, or how you've been getting ready to reenter the workforce. Include any voluntary or community work you've done, seminars or events you've attended, freelancing work you've done, and any other method you've improved your professional abilities. The idea is to make it seem as though you have been involved even in the absence of an official job.

4. Be succinct and leave if necessary.
For various reasons, many people take time off from work. These reasons can occasionally be private and personal affairs that you would rather not discuss.

After addressing the gap and providing an explanation of your activities during that period, return the focus of the interview to your motivation for and suitability for the position. You can accomplish this by asking your interviewer a question after you've responded to their query.

You can choose to say, "I'd prefer not to go into more detail," if the conversation goes in a way that unnerves you. However, I would be quite interested in discussing specifics about my professional experience. You might then go on to provide another tale from your employment history that demonstrates your suitability for the role.

CHAPTER 8

POST-INTERVIEW STRATEGIES

The hiring process's conclusion can be greatly impacted by well-executed post-interview techniques. This chapter offers thorough instructions on how to follow up with the interview, make a good impression, and continue to communicate proactively.

Instant Post-Interview Analysis

Reflection for Immediate Feedback:

Take Note of Important Moments: After the interview, while the details are still fresh in your memory, consider the important questions, moments, and exchanges.

Evaluate Your Work: Analyze your performance, noting your strong qualities and any areas that might need further information or explanation.

Record Unanswered Questions: Make a note of any queries that remained unaddressed or instances where you could strengthen your application with more details.

Following Up: Expressing Gratitude and Reiterating Interest

After a job interview, you should generally send three types of follow-up emails: one to your interviewer(s) right away, one to inquire more if you haven't heard back promptly, and one to maintain contact for networking purposes. Sometimes all you have to do is email the interviewer a quick message of appreciation before they get in touch with you. In other cases, though, you can wait weeks for a potential employer to get back to you following your interview.

A strong follow-up letter can improve your chances of getting recruited and leave a lasting impression. Here are some pointers for crafting an effective follow-up letter following a job interview.

Say "Thank you"

Thank the interviewer for their time and interest at the beginning of your letter. Bring up the position in question as well as the interview date. Show your excitement and gratitude for the chance to work with the organization. Be courteous and professional, but don't forget to be warm and engaging.

Emphasize your credentials.

Next, go over your accomplishments and pertinent abilities with the interviewer, making sure they align with the job requirements. To prove your worth and potential, give concrete instances and figures. Instead of restating your resume in its entirety, concentrate on the highlights that set you apart. Stress how you can help the business achieve its objectives and provide solutions to its issues.

Respond to any issues
This is your chance to clarify and provide an explanation if there was anything you feel you could have done better during the interview or if there was something you forgot to mention. Instead of focusing on your flaws or shortcomings, demonstrate how you can grow from or overcome them. Be truthful and upbeat; don't assign blame or offer justifications.

Reiterate Interest
Sending a follow-up email is more than just expressing gratitude; it's a chance to reaffirm your excitement for the role and the business. Stress how the interview process strengthened your desire to become a member of their team. Mention certain facets of the organization or position that fit your values and career objectives. This demonstrates that you have completed your assigned reading and that you are sincerely looking forward to working with them.

Example of a Follow-Up Email
Subject: I appreciate you coming to see me.

Hi Rose,

I appreciate you spending the time to speak with me this morning. I loved our discussion regarding the Marketing Manager position and gained additional insight into the duties of the position. The way the advertising and marketing departments collaborate seems perfect for achieving objectives and maximizing output.

The marketing manager position seems like a fulfilling career, especially considering the chances for growth and leadership. With my Priston University master's in marketing and over seven years of experience managing marketing teams, I believe I would be a great fit for this role.

I'm excited to talk with you more about this opportunity. Do not hesitate to get in touch with me to set up a re-interview.

I'm grateful.

Hawkins, Michael

Evaluating Job Offers: Negotiation and Decision-Making
There are other considerations besides pay when it comes to accepting a job offer. A thorough assessment of all the variables that affect your overall work satisfaction and professional development is necessary to make the best choice. When assessing a job offer, keep the following points in mind:

Recognize Your Priorities: Before delving into the specifics of the job offer, pause to consider your values, lifestyle choices, and career aspirations. Determine your top priorities, which may include work-life balance, career progression, a particular workplace culture, or a certain location. It will be easier for you to determine whether the employment offer fits with your long-term goals if you are aware of your priorities.

Examine the Compensation Package in Detail: Even if salary plays a big role, it's important to consider other factors as well. Take into account the total remuneration package, which includes any additional benefits such as stock options, bonuses, health insurance, and retirement plans. Examine the package's whole value to see if it satisfies your expectations and budgetary needs.

Examine Opportunities for Career Growth: A job should support your long-term professional development in addition to fulfilling your immediate demands. Evaluate the company's possibilities for expansion. Seek for chances to grow professionally, take on more responsibilities, and learn new skills. In the long run, a profession with a clear route for promotion is probably more gratifying.

Corporate Culture Fit: A key factor in determining job satisfaction is determining how well you'll fit into the corporate culture. Examine the work atmosphere, mission, and values of the organization. Take into account elements like the company's work-life balance policy, communication style, and teamwork philosophy. Making connections with previous or present workers might yield insightful information about the culture of the company.

Work-Life Balance: Achieving a balanced work-life is crucial to general wellness. Examine what the employer expects in terms of flexibility, working hours, and remote work opportunities. Think about how the company's strategy fits into your commitments and way of life. Work-life balance is a key component of job satisfaction and long-term productivity in the workplace.

Evaluate the Job Responsibilities: Make sure the duties and job description fit your interests, abilities, and career objectives. Make sure the position challenges you and lets you take advantage of your strengths. Also, clear up any doubts you may have with the employer. It will be easier to adjust to your new role if you know what is expected of you from the beginning.

Examine the Company's Reputation: Your total work experience might be greatly impacted by a company's reputation. Examine the company's reviews, industry reputation, and web presence. Keep an eye out for any possible warning signs and indicators of staff satisfaction. A company's reputation speaks volumes about its commitment to employee well-being and creates a great work atmosphere.

When Necessary: If any areas need to be adjusted, don't be afraid to negotiate the terms of the employment offer. It shows your dedication to your success when you communicate your requirements and expectations, regardless of the situation—pay, perks, or working conditions. A more favorable agreement can result from a deliberate discussion, which is something that many employers anticipate.

Think About Location and Commute: Your daily commute and place of employment can have a big influence on your quality of life. Think about how long it will take to get to and from work, how far it is, and your options for transportation. Consider whether the place fits your lifestyle and whether it enhances your general well-being.

Seek Professional Advice: You should think about consulting mentors, career coaches, or other industry professionals if you have questions concerning certain components of the job offer. They can offer priceless insights and assist you in impartially balancing the benefits and drawbacks.

To sum up, the process of assessing a job offer extends beyond the first thrill of getting an offer letter. By taking the time to consider a variety of issues, you will be better equipped to make a decision that is consistent with your values and professional aspirations. Choosing the correct work is an important step in your professional journey, which is a constant process of improvement.

Dealing with Rejection: Turning Setbacks into Opportunities

Starting a job hunt is like going on an adventure with ups and downs. Dealing with employment rejections is unavoidably one of the hardest parts. At this point, we get into the specifics of handling rejection, turning obstacles into chances for both professional and personal development, and maintaining an optimistic and driven attitude throughout the job search process.

1.Permit Yourself to Feel
It's quite common to experience disappointment, frustration, or even anger following a rejection. Permit yourself to name these feelings. Suppressing them can eventually result in more severe stress. Permit yourself to be sad about the opportunity you lost.

2. Request Input
Speak with the recruiter or hiring manager and kindly ask for an explanation of your rejection. Positive criticism might give you insightful information about your areas of improvement. Make use of this knowledge to improve your abilities or modify your strategy for upcoming applications.

3. Modify Your Viewpoint
Reframe rejection as an educational opportunity rather than seeing it as a personal failure. Recognize that there are a variety of factors that might affect employment decisions, not all of which are under your control. Pay attention to what you can alter and enhance.

4. Remain tenacious
The secret to finding a job is to be persistent. Never allow one rejection to stop you from going for your professional objectives. Continue networking, applying for jobs, and improving your abilities. It frequently takes several tries

to   achieve   success.

5. Maintain Communication

Even after a rejection, keep up your professional connections and network. The corporate world is smaller than you might imagine, and the contacts you make now could open doors for you later on.

6. Introspection

Give yourself some time to think. Take advantage of the rejection to assess whether the job you applied for fits with your professional ambitions. Think about whether there were any facets of the position or business culture that you might not have been a good fit for.

7. Make New Objectives

Rejection can serve as a motivator to redefine your work path and set new objectives. Evaluate your hobbies, shortcomings, and strengths. Are there any industries or new skills you'd like to go into? Make a plan for the future during this time.

8. Retain your resilience

Being resilient means having the capacity to recover from setbacks. By concentrating on your mental and emotional health, you can cultivate this quality. Take part in joyful activities, take care of yourself, and keep an optimistic mindset.

9. Take into Account Expert Assistance

Consider getting help from a career counselor or therapist if you're having trouble overcoming rejection or if you're feeling down all the time. They can offer advice and resources to assist you in getting through this difficult time.

10. Maintain Perspective

Rejection is a part of life in general, not simply the job search. Everyone experiences disappointments occasionally. Your success ultimately depends on how you handle them.

To sum up, while facing job rejection can be difficult, it can also present a chance for both professional and personal development. You can use a job rejection as a springboard for future success if you ask for and accept feedback, stay persistent, and change the way you see things. Your ideal career can be around the corner if you stay resilient, believe in yourself, and maintain focus on your goals.

CONCLUSION

The ability to perform well in job interviews is a crucial skill for anyone looking to improve professionally and advance in their career. The comprehensive book "How to Answer Interview Questions: Easy and Comprehensive Step-by-Step Guide to Landing a Job" walks readers through the nuances of interview execution, planning, and post-interview tactics. Let's consider the main ideas and lessons learned as we wrap up this enlightening book, which will enable people to become experts in the interview process rather than just answering questions.

Looking Back at the Trip: From Planning to Execution
The book set off on a journey by stressing the value of planning ahead. The interview environment was explained, various interviewer roles were examined, and standard interview formats and structures were familiarized with by the readers. The first few chapters set a solid foundation by emphasizing the value of a professionally written portfolio and resume as well as the need to be aware of any potential red flags.

The chapters delved deeply into the core of the interview process and provided practical guidance on how to construct strong answers, articulate accomplishments, and modify responses to fit the culture of the firm. The guide gave users the confidence to answer a wide range of typical interview questions, like "How do you handle failure?" and "Why should we hire you?" In addition to offering thoughtful comments, readers felt inspired to highlight their value proposition to prospective employers.

Beyond Specialized Interviews: Handling Complexity with Style

The guide devoted an entire chapter to specialized interviews in recognition of the changing nature of interviews. Readers acquired techniques to confidently traverse these distinct settings, regardless of whether they were faced with technical exams, case studies, or industry-specific conversations. The investigation also included group interviews, where cooperation and individuality have to be harmoniously integrated. Techniques for not just standing out but also making a significant contribution in a group environment were offered.

With an emphasis on second and third-round interviews, the journey further guided readers through the advanced stages of the interview process. The techniques for building on past success were outlined as the stakes rose, stressing deeper talent assessments, cultural fit and alignment, and reinforcing key points.

Managing Turnarounds: Become Experts at the Unexpected

The guide's attention to unconventional issues and unexpected events was one of its distinctive features. Understanding that interviews can throw curveballs, readers gained the tools they needed to reply quickly, remain composed under duress, and handle unforeseen difficulties like moral quandaries or pushy interviewers.

The After-Interview Stage: Methodical Pursuit for Enduring Impression

The guide offered a road map for the frequently disregarded post-interview stage when the interview came to an end. It was stressed how to show appreciation by sending out thank-you cards on time. Other techniques included handling constructive or positive criticism, responding to requests for further information, and reiterating important points. The guide included advice on how to stay involved during the decision-making process and negotiate the tricky territory of handling several proposals.

A Comprehensive Strategy for Career Development

This extensive guide encompasses a comprehensive approach to career growth, going beyond the mechanics of answering questions. It acknowledges that presenting qualifications alone won't guarantee success in a job interview; rather, success depends on establishing rapport, proving cultural fit, and adjusting to the fluid nature of business dealings.

Readers were urged to see interviews as chances for real self-expression and ongoing education throughout the entire book. The importance of readiness, introspection, and flexibility in responding to various interview styles was emphasized. A comprehensive grasp of the complex nature of employment interviews was intended by the sub-themes and scenarios that were examined, ranging from group interviews to dealing with unexpected events.

Equipping Readers for Success in the Long Run

The main objective has been to equip readers with the information, abilities, and mindset necessary to not only succeed in interviews but also to start down the path to long-term career success as we draw to a close. The manual is a helpful friend, offering perspectives that go beyond current job search activities.

Interviews for jobs are not one-off occurrences; rather, they represent a continuing story of professional development. Proficiency in interview techniques fosters transferable skills such as effective communication, adaptability, and critical thinking, which are valuable in a variety of professional contexts. This manual aims to develop resilience and self-assurance by encouraging a growth-oriented mindset that welcomes obstacles and sees every encounter as a chance for improvement.

An Ongoing Process of Development

In the ever-changing field of vocations and work, flexibility and a dedication to lifelong learning are critical. This dynamic aspect is reflected in the book's journey, which encourages readers to treat interviews as essential components of an ongoing journey of professional and personal growth rather than as discrete assignments.

May the knowledge, techniques, and confidence that readers have gained be carried with them as they close this guide. May they ace interviews with grace, sincerity, and sincere excitement for the chances that await. Interviews are, after all, about more than just getting a job; they're also about finding the appropriate match, making a meaningful contribution, and moving forward with a career that will influence and fulfill you.

BONUS

SAMPLE INTERVIEW QUESTIONS AND RESPONSES

General Questions:

1.Tell me a little about yourself?
Response: "I work in [Industry/Field] and have [X years] of experience as a [Your Profession]. I effectively [name a task or accomplishment] in my prior position at [Previous Company]. I'm thrilled about the chance to support [Prospective Company] since I am passionate about [particular feature of your field].

2.What prompted you to submit an application for this job?
Response: The reason [Prospective Company] appeals to me is because of its track record for [particular quality or accomplishment]. I think my [relevant talents] match this position's requirements perfectly. I'm excited to offer my knowledge to [Prospective Company] in order to help it accomplish its objectives."

3.How much do you know about our business?

Response:"After carefully examining [Prospective Company], I am impressed by [name a particular accomplishment, endeavor, or quality]." I think your dedication to [specify a particular area, like innovation or customer satisfaction] is consistent with my work ethic."

Behavioral Questions:

4.Tell us about a difficult circumstance you encountered at work and how you resolved it.

Response: "We faced [specific challenge] in my previous role." I took the initiative and [explain your activities], which had [beneficial effect]. I learned from this experience how crucial it is to solve problems proactively and communicate well."

5.Could you give an instance where you showed leadership qualities?
Response: "I had to [explain your duties and actions] while leading a [certain project/team initiative] at [Previous Company]." This experience improved my capacity to lead, assign work efficiently, and complete projects on time."

6.How do you manage pressure and tense deadlines?
Response: "I work best in hectic settings. In my former position, I prioritized work, delegated as needed, and kept lines of communication open with my team to frequently meet deadlines. We were able to regularly

fulfill deadlines and produce high-quality work as a result."

Skills and Qualifications:

7.What technological abilities do you provide for this job?
Response: State that you are "proficient in [certain technical skills, such as software, programming languages]." Because of my knowledge in these fields, I've been able to [list a particular accomplishment or endeavor]. I have faith in my ability to use these abilities in this capacity."

8. How do you keep up with developments and trends in the industry?
Response: "I attend conferences, read trade journals, and engage in pertinent online groups to stay up to date. I'm [name any continuing certifications or courses] because I think learning never stops.

9.Which soft skills do you think are essential for this position?
Response: "I think it's important to collaborate, communicate well, and be flexible. I've refined these abilities in past positions via [name particular experiences]. These attributes, along with my technological know-how, make me a strong candidate for this job."

Career and Goal-oriented Questions:

10.In five years, where do you see yourself?
Response: "I hope to have advanced in my job by [specify specific career goals] in five years. I anticipate myself playing a major leadership role in [Prospective Company's] growth and am dedicated to lifelong learning."

11.What about this field or industry appeals to you?
Response: "I am particularly excited about the dynamic nature of [mention any trends or advancements] because I am passionate about [specific aspect of the industry/field]." One of my main motivations is to help this industry flourish and innovate."

12.How do you approach skill improvement and professional development?
Response: "I take the initiative to advance my career. I frequently take part in industry conferences, webinars, and workshops. I also ask mentors for their opinions, and I'm working on [name any particular project to improve your skills right now]."

Company-specific Questions:

13.What makes you the right candidate for this job?
Response: "I offer a special blend of [specify particular abilities, encounters, or attributes] that meet the requirements of this role. My potential to contribute

significantly to [Prospective Company] is demonstrated by my track record of [list pertinent achievements].

14.What distinguishes our business from competitors in the field, in your opinion?

Response: "What distinguishes [Prospective Company] is its [specify a special feature, such as an inventive strategy or a dedication to sustainability]." This is in line with my principles, and I'm excited to add value to a company that leads in [certain area]."

15.In what way could you enhance the culture of our business?

Response: "I cherish teamwork, candid communication, and a happy workplace. I have actively participated in team-building exercises and efforts that support a strong workplace culture in my past positions. I'm excited to introduce this way of thinking to [Prospective Company]."

Problem-solving and Critical Thinking:

16.Describe an instance in which you had to come up with an original answer.

Response: "In a prior position, we dealt with [particular difficulty], and I suggested [explain your original idea]. This not only fixed the problem but also [list benefits, such increased productivity or cost savings]."

17.How do you go about resolving challenging issues?

Response:I break down difficult issues into smaller, more manageable parts, carry out in-depth analyses, and work with others in my team to solve them. In my past employment, this methodical approach has enabled me to successfully navigate hurdles."

18.Could you provide an instance where you had to alter how you approached a problem?

Response: "In a project at [Prior Company], the first approaches were not producing the expected outcomes. I aggressively reassessed our plan, solicited feedback from the group, and made necessary adjustments. This adaptability produced a better project result."

Collaboration and Teamwork:

19.How do you resolve disputes or conflicts within a team?

Response: "I think it's important to communicate openly. When disagreements emerge, I start a productive conversation to learn about other people's viewpoints. By identifying points of agreement and working toward solutions that are advantageous to the group and project, I have effectively arbitrated disputes."

20. Give the details of a productive group project you worked on.

Response:"In my prior position, I was a major contributor to a team project where we [explain the project and your role]. Our combined efforts produced [name particular successes or favorable results], demonstrating the value of productive teamwork."

21. How can you make sure that team members communicate effectively?

Response: "I place a high priority on holding frequent team meetings where everyone may voice updates and worries. In addition, I promote an open-door policy and effectively use communication tools to create an atmosphere where team members feel free to share their thoughts."

22.Failure and Adversity: Could you describe a professional setback you had and how you overcame it?

Response: "We encountered [particular setback] in a prior capacity, which taught me [list lessons learned]. I was proactive and [explain activities performed], which resulted in [improvement or favorable outcome]. My capacity for resilience and problem-solving was enhanced by this encounter."

23.What lessons have you learned from failure, and how do you respond to it?

Response: "I see failure as a chance to learn and improve. When I encounter obstacles, I consider the underlying reasons, ask for input, and devise ways to get better. My professional development has been greatly aided by this iterative procedure."

Time management & Prioritization

24. How do you prioritize your many responsibilities and meet deadlines?

Response: "I rank things according to their significance and urgency. I use resources such as [name particular resources or methods] to develop a methodical plan that guarantees timely completion. I can adjust to shifting priorities with the support of regular check-ins and modifications."

25.Could you give an instance of a moment when you had to rearrange your workload?
Response: "Unexpected priorities came up in former employment that needed to be attended to right away. I rearranged my workload, gave things to others where I could, and kept open lines of communication with all parties involved. I was able to successfully meet the additional demands because of my adaptability."

Future Input into the Business:

26.In your first ninety days in this position, what goals do you have?
Response: "I will be concentrating on [naming specific objectives, such as comprehending team dynamics and participating in ongoing projects] for the first ninety days." My objectives are to become part of the team as soon as possible, pinpoint areas that need work, and provide real value to [Prospective Company]."

27.In this position, how do you intend to stay current on industry developments?
Response: "In [industry/field], staying current is crucial." I intend to interact with trade journals, go to pertinent

conferences, and take part in networking events for professionals. I'm also open to mentorship possibilities to broaden my understanding of the sector."

Diversity and Inclusion

28.What are some strategies for fostering these concepts in the workplace?
Reaction: "I actively support inclusive policies and a diverse and inclusive workplace by [naming specific actions, such as attending diversity training sessions]." I think that having a variety of viewpoints fosters innovation and a healthy work environment."

29.How do you respond when you witness or encounter discrimination?
Response: "I deal with discrimination in a proactive manner by [describing actions, such as reporting incidents, helping impacted colleagues]." I'm dedicated to helping to create an atmosphere at work where everyone feels appreciated and respected since I firmly believe in it."

Final Questions:

30.Do you want to ask us any questions?
"Yeah, I'd like to know more about [a particular division within the company, the composition of the team, or upcoming initiatives." I'm also interested in [discuss any current projects or advancements]."

Keep in mind that they are templates; therefore it's important to customize them according to your background and the particular demands of the position. Practice your responses to these questions as well to improve your confidence and mannerisms in the real interview.